HAIKU

Books by Richard Wright

Uncle Tom's Children
Native Son
12 Million Black Voices
Black Boy
The Outsider
Savage Holiday
Black Power
The Color Curtain
Pagan Spain
White Man, Listen!
The Long Dream
Eight Men
Lawd Today
Richard Wright Reader
American Hunger
Rite of Passage

HAIKU
The Last Poems
of an American Icon

RICHARD WRIGHT

Edited with Notes and Afterword by
Yoshinobu Hakutani and Robert L. Tener

Introduction by Julia Wright

ARCADE PUBLISHING • NEW YORK

Of course, I don't want anything to happen to me, but if it does my friends will know exactly where it comes from. If I tell you these things, it is to let you know what happens. So far as the Americans are concerned, I'm worse than a Communist, for my work falls like a shadow across their policy in Asia and Africa. That's the problem: they've asked me time and again to work for them, but I'd die first. . . . But they try to divert me with all kinds of foolish tricks.

In a remarkable book, *Alien Ink*, Natalie Robbins chillingly reminds us that we will never know what American masterpieces were nipped in the bud because of the cold war blighting of creative powers unable to blossom. But my father's own response to this onslaught against the deepest springs of his genius was to continue to spin these poems of light out of the gathering darkness.

But, the wound that went the deepest, the piece of news that hit him by far the hardest, was the death of his mother, Ella, in January 1959, the very same month a writer he highly admired, Albert Camus, was killed in an automobile accident.

I do not remember my father uttering a single word after a telegram announced the passing of a mother he had written about so heartrendingly in *Black Boy*. Even his letter instructing his literary agent, Paul Reynolds, to advance a small sum for the funeral, given his dwindling bank account,

HAIKU

The Last Poems
of an ***American Icon***

RICHARD WRIGHT

Edited with Notes and Afterword by
Yoshinobu Hakutani and Robert L. Tener

Introduction by Julia Wright

ARCADE PUBLISHING • NEW YORK

Arcade Publishing books may be purchased in bulk at special
discounts for sales promotion, corporate gifts, fund-raising, or
educational purposes. Special editions can also be created to
specifications. For details, contact the Special Sales Department,
Arcade Publishing, 307 West 36th Street, 11th Floor, New York,
NY 10018 or arcade@skyhorsepublishing.com.

Arcade Publishing® is a registered trademark of Skyhorse
Publishing, Inc.®, a Delaware corporation.

Visit our website at www.arcadepub.com.

10 9 8 7

Library of Congress Cataloging-in-Publication Data is available
on file.

ISBN: 978-1-61145-349-2

Printed in China

CONTENTS

INTRODUCTION

The haiku you are about to read were written during my father's French exile, almost forty years ago, throughout the last eighteen months or so of his life. That they should finally be published as Richard Wright wanted them to be read is definitely a literary event and offers some exciting clues to a biographical enigma: how the creator of the inarticulate, frightened, and enraged Bigger Thomas ended up leaving us some of the most tender, unassuming, and gentle lines in African-American poetry.

One of my last memories of my father during the summer and autumn months before he died is his crafting of thousands of haiku. He was never without his haiku binder under his arm. He wrote them everywhere, at all hours: in bed as he slowly recovered from a year-long, grueling battle against amebic dysentery; in cafés and restaurants where he counted syllables on napkins; in the country in a writing community owned by French friends, *Le Moulin d'Andé*. Although he had at last overcome the amoebas, he was often inexplicably exhausted and feverish in those days as he worked on the revisions of the uncompleted *Island of*

Hallucination and typed up the early chapters of another unfinished novel, *A Father's Law*.

My father's law in those days revolved around the rules of haiku writing, and I remember how he would hang pages and pages of them up, as if to dry, on long metal rods strung across the narrow office area of his tiny sunless studio in Paris, like the abstract still-life photographs he used to compose and develop himself at the beginning of his Paris exile. I also recall how one day he tried to teach me how to count the syllables: "Julia, you can write them, too. It's always five, and seven and five—like math. So you can't go wrong." Back then I was an immature eighteen-year-old and, worried as we all were by his drastic weight loss (the haiku must have been light to carry) and the strange slowness of his recovery, we did not immediately establish a link between his daily poetic exercises and his ailing health. Today I know better. I believe his haiku were self-developed antidotes against illness, and that breaking down words into syllables matched the shortness of his breath, especially on the bad days when his inability to sit up at the typewriter restricted the very breadth of writing.

Today, I also wonder whether these little poetic gems did not serve another deeper purpose as my father attempted to bring closure to the numerous mournings he experienced during the same period. In 1958 he lost his favorite editor and friend, Ed Aswell. And in September of the following year it was the turn of George Padmore, a close friend with whom he had excitedly planned another trip to Africa. Padmore's sudden death was all the more a shock because my father had sold his beloved country retreat (recaptured in many of these haiku) to move our whole family to England, where "Uncle" George resided. The British Home Office coarsely rejected his immigration application shortly after his friend's death. And so loss followed upon loss. A few weeks before Richard died, he learned of the suicide of a young Danish girl, Bente Heeris, who had asked him during a brief correspondence to dissuade her from her wish to end her life.

And there were other disquieting areas of turmoil. My father's open querying of American counterintelligence tactics targeting radical black expatriates, his research plans around racial tensions on U.S. Army bases in Europe as part of the gathering of background material for *Island of Hallucination*, his attempt to protect his friend and confidant, Ollie Harrington, from the ambushes of cold war politics, all these interests and loyalties culminated in the realization that he himself was being increasingly monitored during those last months. This fact, ascribed by so many critics to his "paranoia," was to be eerily confirmed, years later, by the contents of intelligence reports released under the Freedom of Information Act. In fact, the decision to maintain Richard Wright on the National Security Index was more or less contemporary to his haiku period. As my father wrote so lucidly to another trusted friend, Margrit de Sablonière, on March 30, 1960:

Of course, I don't want anything to happen to me, but if it does my friends will know exactly where it comes from. If I tell you these things, it is to let you know what happens. So far as the Americans are concerned, I'm worse than a Communist, for my work falls like a shadow across their policy in Asia and Africa. That's the problem: they've asked me time and again to work for them, but I'd die first. . . . But they try to divert me with all kinds of foolish tricks.

In a remarkable book, *Alien Ink*, Natalie Robbins chillingly reminds us that we will never know what American masterpieces were nipped in the bud because of the cold war blighting of creative powers unable to blossom. But my father's own response to this onslaught against the deepest springs of his genius was to continue to spin these poems of light out of the gathering darkness.

But, the wound that went the deepest, the piece of news that hit him by far the hardest, was the death of his mother, Ella, in January 1959, the very same month a writer he highly admired, Albert Camus, was killed in an automobile accident.

I do not remember my father uttering a single word after a telegram announced the passing of a mother he had written about so heartrendingly in *Black Boy*. Even his letter instructing his literary agent, Paul Reynolds, to advance a small sum for the funeral, given his dwindling bank account, was strangely short and emotionless. To the teenager I then was, his silence passed over our household like a long, dark cloud. But today I see things otherwise. The haiku enabled him to mourn a mother whose physical absence from his life had begun way before her death—but whose invisible presence haunted all his exile writings. His vow not to break the fast of self-imposed exile could never entirely suppress his mother-hunger and the yearning for the world of childhood she had given him. A form of poetry which links seasons of the soul with nature's cycle of moods enabled him to reach out to the black boy part of himself still stranded in a South that continued to live in his dreams. With the haiku, a self-nurturing could begin, albeit so close to his own death.

My father had come a long way. Back in the forties, he had written in his journal how much he disliked the countryside because it reminded him of the physical hunger he had experienced as a poor black child in one of the world's most fertile landscapes. And so these haiku not only helped him place the volcanic experience of mourning under the self-control of closely counted syllables, but also enabled him to come to terms with the difficult beauty of the earth in which his mother would be laid to rest.

For Richard Wright, hunger and beauty were once upon a time terrifying and ravaging. But writing these poems kept him spiritually afloat. Some of us will even find these deceptively simple patterns of syllables tap-dancing in our minds long after they are read. They are Richard

Wright's poetry of loss and retrieval, of temperate joy and wistful humor, of exile and fragments of a dreamed return. They lie somewhere in that transitional twilight area between the loss for words and the few charmed syllables that can heal the loss.

Julia Wright
Connecticut, 1998

EDITORS' NOTE

In 1960 Wright selected under the title *This Other World: Projections in the Haiku Manner* 817 out of about four thousand haiku he had composed. The manuscript consists of a title page and eighty-two pages, page 1 containing the first seven haiku and each of the rest ten. The manuscript, dated 1960, is deposited among the Wright collection in the Beinecke Rare Book and Manuscript Library, Yale University, New Haven, Connecticut. Each of the haiku in this edition is numbered consecutively 1 through 817.

In editing the text for this volume we have emended obvious spelling errors, but retained Wright's typography regarding spelling, capitalization, hyphenation, and punctuation as it appeared in the original manuscript.

Completing this book would have been impossible without the help and cooperation we have received from many sources. First, we would like to express our gratitude to Mrs. Ellen Wright, who suggested in her letter to Robert L. Tener back in 1986 that we might work with her and write an introduction and notes.

Unfortunately, Wright's unpublished haiku had been restricted till quite recently. We would also like to name Patricia C. Willis, Curator of American Literature, of the Beinecke Rare Book and Manuscript Library, Yale University, where the manuscript of Wright's haiku is housed, who allowed Yoshinobu Hakutani to read it in its entirety in the spring of 1991.

It also was an honor and pleasure for Yoshinobu Hakutani to meet Julia Wright, Wright's daughter, along with Mrs. Wright, when he attended the African-American Writers conference held in Paris in February 1992. He talked with them about our work in progress.

In the course of the work, Yoshinobu Hakutani has benefited from a research grant and several grants-in-aid provided by the Kent State University Research Council.

We have also been encouraged by Michel Fabre over the years to complete the project. And it has been assisted by Michiko Hakutani and Carolyn Tener from the beginning.

Y. H. and R. L. T.

EDITORS' NOTE

HAIKU

1

I am nobody:
A red sinking autumn sun
   Took my name away.

2

For you, O gulls,
I order slaty waters
   And this leaden sky!

3

Keep straight down this block,
Then turn right where you will find
   A peach tree blooming.

4

Sweep away the clouds
And let a dome of blue sky
   Give this sea a name!

5

I give permission
For this slow spring rain to soak
The violet beds.

6

Follow wherever
The tree branches make arches
In the torrid sun.

7

Make up your mind, Snail!
You are half inside your house,
And halfway out!

8

O finicky cat,
Forgive me for this spring rain
That disgusts you so!

Steep with deep sweetness,
O You White Magnolias,
 This still torpid night!

"Shut up, you crickets!
How can I hear what my wife
 Is saying to me?"

You moths must leave now;
I am turning out the light
 And going to sleep.

"Oh, Mr. Scarecrow,
Stop waving your arms about
 Like a foreigner!"

13

I would like a bell
Tolling in this soft twilight
Over willow trees.

14

I grant to sparrows
The telegraph wires that brought
Me such good tidings!

15

O Anvil, be beaten,
Bear all the bitter blows till
The spring sun goes down!

16

All right, You Sparrows;
The sun has set and you can now
Stop your chattering!

17

In a misty rain
A butterfly is riding
The tail of a cow.

18

Sparrow's excrement
Becomes quickly powdery
On sizzling pavements.

19

A summer barnyard:
Swishing tails of twenty cows
Twitching at the flies.

20

The dog's violent sneeze
Fails to rouse a single fly
On his mangy back.

21

On winter mornings
The candle shows faint markings
Of the teeth of rats.

22

With a twitching nose
A dog reads a telegram
On a wet tree trunk.

23

On muddy puddles
Of the hoof-tramped farmyard,
Flashing glints of spring.

24

The webs of spiders
Sticking to my sweaty face
In the dusty woods.

25

A horse is pissing
In the snow-covered courtyard
In the morning sun.

26

From a red tile roof
A cat is licking beads of dew
In a humid dawn.

27

Across the river
Huge dark sheets of cool spring rain
Falling on a town.

28

In the summer haze:
Behind magnolias,
Faint sheets of lightning.

29

A huge drift of snow
Blocks the narrow pathway to
The little toy shop.

30

A bloody knife blade
Is being licked by a cat
At hog-killing time.

31

In the falling snow
A laughing boy holds out his palms
Until they are white.

32

Just enough of light
In this lofty autumn sky
To turn the lake black.

33

Just enough of snow
For a boy's finger to write
   His name on the porch.

34

The sound of the rain,
Blotted out now and then
   By a sticky cough.

35

Venturing outdoors,
The children walk timidly,
   Respecting the snow.

36

A brick tenement
Is receiving furniture
   In a light snowfall.

37

Past the window pane
A solitary snowflake
Spins furiously.

38

That abandoned house,
With its yard of fallen leaves,
In the setting sun.

39

A soft wind at dawn
Lifts one dry leaf and lays it
Upon another.

40

In gray winter light,
Dead flies fill the window sill
Of a musty room.

Just before dawn,
When the streets are deserted,
A light spring rain.

42

Seen from a hilltop,
Shadowy in winter rain,
A man and his mule.

43

What river is that
Meandering through the mist
In fields of young corn?

44

A man leaves his house
And walks around his winter fields
And then goes back in.

45

As though for always,
Each petal lit by the sun,—
Apple blossoms!

46

A spring mountain holds
The foundations of a house
Long since tumbled down.

47

The spring lingers on
In the scent of a damp log
Rotting in the sun.

48

A bursting ripe plum
Forms a pool upon a leaf
From which sparrows drink.

49

Burning autumn leaves,
I yearn to make the bonfire
    Bigger and bigger.

50

One magnolia
Landed upon another
    In the dew-wet grass.

51

As the sun goes down,
A green melon splits open
    And juice trickles out.

52

Gazing at her face
Reflected in the spring pond,
    The girl grimaces.

53

A sparrow's feather
On a barb of rusty wire
In the sizzling heat.

54

A September rain
Tumbling down in drops so big
They wobble as they fall.

55

Shaking the water
Off his dripping body,
The dog swims again.

56

The cool green melon
Made me trace my forefinger
Along its whole length.

57

Sleety rain at night
Seasoning swelling turnips
With a tangy taste.

58

Heaps of black cherries
Glittering with drops of rain
In the evening sun.

59

Gusty autumn rain
Swinging a yellow lantern
Over wet cattle.

60

Sun is glinting on
A washerwoman's black arms
In cold creek water.

61

The melting snowflakes
Are wetting the brown horse's back
Darker than his flanks.

62

A lance of spring sun
Falls upon the moldy oats
In a musty barn.

63

From far, far off,
From over the leaden sea,
The call of a ship.

64

The harbor at dawn:
The faint scent of oranges
On gusts of March wind.

65

A December wind
Swept the sky clean of clouds
And froze the lake still.

66

A freezing night wind
Wafts the scent of frying fish
From the waterfront.

67

The day is so long
That even noisy sparrows
Fall strangely silent.

68

A chill Spanish dawn:
Vapor from the blood of a
Freshly slaughtered bull.

69

Whose town did you leave,
O wild and droning spring rain,
And where do you go?

70

At the water's edge,
Amid drifting brown leaves,
A dead bloated fish.

71

It is not the sun,
But the spring rain that beats loose
The rose's petals.

72

Droning into the room,
The wasp circles angrily,
Then hums slowly out.

73

Naked to the sky,
A village without a name
In the setting sun.

74

Midnight is striking:
In a cold drizzle of rain
Two men are parting.

75

Spring begins shyly
With one hairpin of green grass
In a flower pot.

76

The path in the woods
Is barred by spider webs
Beaded with spring rain.

77

Dewdrop joins dewdrop
Till a petal holds a pool
Reflecting its rose.

78

An apple blossom
Trembling on a sunlit branch
From the weight of bees.

79

Spring arrives stealthily:
Scaly flecks of peeling paint
On a whitewashed wall.

80

After the rainstorm,
A tendril of Wisteria
Peeps over the wall.

81

The river ripples
From the caressing shadows
Of a willow tree.

82

A butterfly makes
The sunshine even brighter
With fluttering wings.

83

A falling petal
Strikes one floating on a pond,
And they both sink.

84

On the pond's green scum
A yellow butterfly lights;
And then there are two.

85

Upon a pine tree,
A snail slides out of its shell
To witness the spring.

86

The wings of a bee,
Tarnishing the smooth whiteness
Of a magnolia.

87

Meticulously,
The cat licks dew-wet cobwebs
From between his toes.

88

The cat's shining eyes
Are remarkably blue
Beside the jonquils.

89

In the hot kitchen
A feather drags its shadow
Over steaming rice.

90

How the rain washes
Wrinkled skins of writhing worms
To a tender pink!

91

Just enough of wind
To agitate soundlessly
The maple tree leaves.

92

A caterpillar
Has entrapped wet spider webs
Upon its short hairs.

93

Leaving its nest,
The sparrow sinks a second,
Then opens its wings.

94

A snail hesitates,
Contracting one of its horns
In a gust of wind.

95

Like a fishhook,
The sunflower's long shadow
Hovers in the lake.

96

You could see warm wind
Drying wet wisps of her hair
About her forehead.

97

In the setting sun,
Each tree bud is clinging fast
To drying raindrops.

98

It took five seconds
For the barefoot boy's wet tracks
To dry on the porch.

99

Where the tree's shadow
Lingers on the macadam,
Traces of spring rain.

100

Just enough of rain
To set black ants a-swimming
Over yellow sand.

101

Quickly vanishing,
The first drops of summer rain
On an old wood door.

102

On the pond's bottom
The faint shadow of a fish
Flitting on white sand.

103

Just enough of rain
To bring the smell of silk
From umbrellas.

104

Trembling on the wall,
A yellow water shadow
From the lake outside.

105

A cow chews her cud
As flimsy heaps of snowflakes
Sift from off her horns.

106

Beads of quicksilver
On a black umbrella:
Moonlit April rain.

107

Just enough of snow
To make the back of each cow
Vivid in the dusk.

108

From the scarecrow's sleeve
A tiny green leaf unfolds
On an oaken arm.

109

On a pulpy log,
An ant pauses in the sun
And waves its feelers.

110

I laid down my book:
A tendril of Wisteria
Encircling my leg.

111

With shy yellow smiles,
Baby pumpkins are hiding
Under yellow leaves.

112

And though level full,
The petal holds its dew,
And without trembling.

113

A twisting tendril
Tilting off into sunshine,
    Winding on itself.

114

Not even the sun
Can make oak tree leaves as green
    As the starlight does.

115

Why do I listen
To the muttering thunder
    This night of spring?

116

A lone lance of sun
Spotlighting a lone fly
    Washing one blue wing.

117

The crow flew so fast
That he left his lonely caw
Behind in the fields.

118

For some strange reason
Sparrows are congregating
In an old rose bush.

119

On a clapboard house,
An old oak tree's shadow fades
In the spring sunset.

120

Crying and crying,
Melodious strings of geese
Passing a graveyard.

121

The consumptive man,
Who lives in the room next door,
Did not cough today.

122

And what do *you* think,
O still and awesome spider,
Of this summer rain?

123

And now this thing too:
A drunken girl vomiting
In the autumn rain.

124

Persistent magpies
Are pecking amid hot grasses
At one blue glass eye.

125

Yellow petals gone,
The sunflower looks blankly
    In a drizzling rain.

126

Yet another dawn
Upon yellowing leaves
    And my sleepless eyes.

127

Why does the blindman
Stop so still for a second
    In the drizzling dusk?

128

This autumn drizzle
Is our bond with other eyes
    That can see no more.

129

This winding dirt path
Ends in a tangle of thorns
In the autumn mist.

130

A long autumn day:
A wind blowing from the west,
But none from the east.

131

Is this the dirt road,
Winding through windy trees,
That I must travel?

132

What stranger is that
Walking in the winter rain
And looking this way?

133

Is there some design
In these deep random raindrops
Drying in the dust?

134

One autumn evening
A stranger enters a village
And passes on through.

135

Six cows are grazing;
The seventh stands near a fence,
Staring into space.

136

That road is empty,
The one leading into hills
In autumn twilight.

137

A pregnant black rat
Poking in a paper bag
In a purple dawn.

138

Upon the roof's edge,
A cat in autumn moonlight
Contemplates the road.

139

Pulling him ahead,
The blindman's dog takes a path
Between summer graves.

140

A spring pond as calm
As the lips of the dead girl
Under its water.

141

An autumn sunset:
A buzzard sails slowly past,
　　Not flapping its wings.

142

A wounded sparrow
Sinks in clear cold lake water,
　　Its eyes still open.

143

Why is hail so wild,
Bouncing so frighteningly,
　　Only to lie so still?

144

Amidst the flowers
A China clock is ticking
　　In the dead man's room.

145

A bright glowing moon
Pouring out its radiance
    Upon tall tombstones.

146

In a silent room
A feather rises slowly
    And floats in the heat.

147

It is without taste,
Or am I a stranger here—?
    These drops of spring dew.

148

As still as death is,
Under a circling buzzard,
    An autumn village.

149

I had long felt that
Those sprawling black railroad tracks
Would bring down this snow.

150

Late one winter night
I saw a skinny scarecrow
Gobbling slabs of meat.

151

The harvest is in:
The trees on the distant hills
Have been bought by clouds.

152

After seven days,
The corpse in the coffin
Turned on its side.

153

The snow has melted,
And now all the fields belong
To the railroad tracks.

154

Standing in spring rain,
The hitchhiker has a stance
That nobody trusts.

155

Empty railroad tracks:
A train sounds in the spring hills
And the rails leap with life.

156

A winter evening:
The black craggy mountains
Are calling down rain.

157

The drumming of sleet
Against the roof and windows
Brightly fans the fire.

158

A train crashes past:
A butterfly still as stone
On the humid earth.

159

In the melting snow
That is tracked into the house
Is one green grass blade.

160

The barking of dogs
Is deepening the yellow
Of the sunflowers.

161

The call of a bird
Sends a solid cake of snow
Sliding off a roof.

162

Deep green melons
Anchoring gigantic clouds,
Dyeing them purple.

163

As the music stops,
Flooding strongly to the ear,
The sound of spring rain.

164

I slept so long and sound,
But I did not know why until
I saw the snow outside.

165

The caw of a crow,
Telling of a taut white sail
On the flashing river.

166

The snow on the bank
Stains the river water black
Under a blue sky.

167

Bulging yellow clouds:
Between peals of spring thunder,
Deep white silences.

168

Beyond a railroad,
A river and a sunset
In the April rain.

169

Turning on the light
The drip-drip of the spring rain
Lessens in the dawn.

170

A spring haze wipes out
The brick wall between my house
And the hillside graves.

171

With indignation
A little girl spanks her doll,—
The sound of spring rain.

172

The scarecrow's old hat
Was flung by the winter wind
Into a graveyard.

173

The first day of spring:
The snow on the far mountains,
Brighter than ever.

174

Merciful autumn
Tones down the shabby curtains
Of my rented room.

175

Coming from the woods,
A bull has a lilac sprig
Dangling from a horn.

176

Winter rain at night
Sweetening the taste of bread
And spicing the soup.

177

Spring dawn is glinting
On a dew-wet garbage can
In a city street.

178

From an icy quay:
When her ship heaves into sight,
The sea disappears.

179

The summer moonlight
Gleams upon a blacksmith's forge,
And cools red embers.

180

The elevator
Lifts him up twenty stories,—
A bright summer sea!

181

When the train had stopped,
A coffin was unloaded
Amid steam and smoke.

182

A bright window pane
With one slowly crawling fly
Against a still cloud.

183

All the city's bells
Clang deafeningly this midnight,
Frightening the New Year!

184

No birds are flying;
The tree leaves are still as stone,—
An autumn evening.

185

The sound of the wind
Is shaping long drifts of snow
On a mountain ridge.

186

From these warm spring days,
I can still see her sad face
In its last autumn.

187

In an old woodshed
The long points of icicles
Are sharpening the wind.

188

The night must be long
For even a yellow moon
Over fields of snow.

189

Does the willow know
That the tip of its drooping branch
Is touching the ice?

190

Factory whistles
Bring flurries of fat snow
In a winter dawn.

191

Little boys tossing
Stones at a guilty scarecrow
In a snowy field.

192

Even the sparrows
Are attempting to thaw out
The frozen scarecrow.

193

Standing patiently,
The horse grants the snowflakes
A home on his back.

194

A cracking tree limb
Intensifies the starlight
Upon blue-white snow.

195

O Blacksmith's Hammer,
How hot and hard must you pound
To change this cold wind?

196

Tossing all day long,
The cold sea now sleeps deeply
On a bed of stars.

197

A blacksmith's hammer
Beating the silver moon thin
On a cool spring night.

198

The first day of spring:
A servant's hips shake as she
Wipes a mirror clean.

199

The shuddering flank
Of a bull in the spring rain
Calls down the thunder.

200

A silent spring wood:
A crow opens its sharp beak
And creates a sky.

201

Over spring mountains
A star ends the paragraph
Of a thunderstorm.

202

A cock's shrill crow
Is driving the spring dawn stars
From out of the sky.

203

Did somebody call?
Looking over my shoulder:
Massive spring mountains.

204

To see the spring sky,
A doll in a store window
Leans far to one side.

205

As my delegate,
With joints stiff with winter cold,
The first ant of spring.

206

As the spring snow melts,
All the village houses are
Huddling together.

207

The shouts of children
Billowing window curtains
On spring's first day.

208

A horse gives a neigh
And shakes down the first spring rain
With his tossing mane.

209

As my delegate,
The spring wind has its fingers
In a young girl's hair.

210

The sprinting spring rain
Knocks upon a wooden door
That has just been shut.

211

A fleeing white fence
Is ripping the moon away
From the April clouds.

212

From the skyscraper,
All the bustling streets converge
Towards a spring sea.

213

Fields of young barley
Under ten billion hailstones
In the April sun.

214

While plowing the earth,
All my crows are visiting
A neighboring farm.

215

Legions of crows
Are busily unplanting
The farmer's barley.

216

The trilling sparrows
Sound as if they too had got
A letter today!

217

Surely that spring moon,
So yellow and so fragile,
    Will crack on a cloud!

218

A far-away fog
Is troubling the evening star
    Above a spring hill.

219

Enough of dawn light
To show pearly pear blossom
    Burning from within.

220

The cathedral bell
Is now rocking the spring moon
    Upon the river.

RICHARD WRIGHT

221

Even the horse looks
At the duck and her ducklings
Following in line.

222

Holding too much rain,
The tulip stoops and spills it,
Then straightens again.

223

A highway of black ants
Diagonally bisecting
A sun-hot white wall.

224

While convalescing,
The red roses have no smell,
Gently mocking me.

225

Every sandgrain
Of the vast sunlit desert
    Hears the snake crawling.

226

Like a spreading fire,
Blossoms leap from tree to tree
    In a blazing spring.

227

In the damp darkness,
Croaking frogs are belching out
    The scent of magnolias.

228

The sudden thunder
Startles the magnolias
    To a deeper white.

Fierce sunflowers
Have forced every cloud fleece
Out of the hot sky.

230

A lone cricket's cry
Slices a sliver of moon
And scatters the stars.

231

At the dying sun,
Glaring with greedy black eyes,
Tiger-lilies.

232

A descending moon
Commanding crickets to sing
Louder in the woods.

233

The magnolias
Waft their misty scent skywards,
  Obscuring the moon.

234

O black rattlesnake,
Why in all hell did you choose
  This path to sleep in?

235

The caw of a crow
Draws a diagonal line
  Across a field of corn.

236

The dusty petals
Of ferocious sunflowers
  Hold the rain at bay.

237

The caw of a crow
Loops over a sunburnt hill
And fills a valley.

238

The crows are boasting
Of having driven the sun
Down a murky sky.

239

Sitting in the park,
Hearing the sound of an axe
Rippling the lake.

240

In a red sunset
A frog commands the night wind
To roll out a moon.

241

A blindman's eyebrows
Condensing the autumn fog
Into beads of light.

242

The darting fire-flies
Are dragging the river along
To where the sun went down.

243

Leaving the doctor,
The whole world looks different
This autumn morning.

244

As day tumbles down,
The setting sun's signature
Is written in red.

245

Harvesting over,
The empty fields are yearning
Toward a gray sky.

246

In a murky dawn
The faint moon is sucking smoke
Out of chimneytops.

247

The wheat has been cut,
And now a blue-gray mountain
Is haunting the lake.

248

Harvesting over,
The empty fields have been bought
By the horizon.

249

The sleet stops droning
And the still silence forbids
Even the sun to shine.

250

Even toy soldiers
Perspire with weariness
In the autumn mist.

251

A rooster's sharp crow
Punctures a gray dawn sky,
Letting out spring rain.

252

Fiery apples
Are searing the tree leaves
And singeing the grass.

253

From a tenement,
The blue jazz of a trumpet
   Weaving autumn mists.

254

I almost forgot
To hang up an autumn moon
   Over the mountain.

255

The shore slips away
From the melancholy ship
   In an autumn mist.

256

Crying of the past,
Cascading upon my roof,
   A cold winter rain.

257

A wisp of white smoke:
Out of a widow's chimney
Winter is rising.

258

A dog's blood-red bark
Lights up the summer forest
And blanches the moon.

259

Sounds of red and black:
Rain beating upon the river
And upon tree leaves.

260

The shimmering heat
Undulates the drooping flag
Atop the courthouse.

261

A night of spring stars:
Waves breaking beyond the wall
Have a dark blue sound.

262

After the parade,
After all the flags are gone,
The snow is whiter.

263

A departing ship
Sends forth a deep-throated tone
That turns the sea blue.

264

Even the cat smiles
When the hen swallows water
With back-tilted head.

265

The blue of this sky
Sounds so loud that it can be heard
Only with our eyes.

266

The wings of crows
Are scudding the purple clouds
And misting the fields.

267

The cock's ready crow
Is as dark as autumn dawn
With edges of white.

268

No star and no moon:
A dog is barking whitely
In the winter night.

RICHARD WRIGHT

269

The swaying lanterns
Under the magnolias
   Glow with sweet scent.

270

Lifting the lantern,
The scent of plums on the tree
   Became more fragrant.

271

The sharper the scent
Of magnolia blossoms,
   The hotter the sun.

272

They smelt like roses;
But when I put on the light,
   They were violets.

273

One, two, three June bugs;
Now there are seven June bugs
More of torrid heat.

274

The valley is full
Of the scent of violets
Scattered by spring rain.

275

The smell of sunny snow
Is swelling the icy air,—
The world grows bigger.

276

Just enough of moon
To make the smell of apples
Light up the orchard.

277

The chill autumn dusk
Grows colder as yellow lights
Come on in skyscrapers.

278

Streaks of fire-flies
Freezing the magnolias
As white as ice.

279

This September rain
Is much colder than the wind
That sweeps it along.

280

The scent of an orange
By an ice-coated window
In a rocking train.

281

An October night:
Rising from rain-wet shingles,
  The cool scent of pine.

282

The screech of shovels,
Scooping snow off the sidewalks
  Deepens the cold.

283

By night: "O how cold!"
But by daylight: "O how hot!"
  Chanting peach blossoms.

284

The metallic taste
Of a siren cutting through
  The hot summer air.

285

The grate of a saw
Hacking into a slab of ice
Is a death rattle.

286

With intense effort
The blindman's eyes are squinting:
How bitter the cold!

287

The sun is as hot
As the big red carbuncle
On the fat man's neck.

288

A freezing morning:
I left a bit of my skin
On the broomstick handle.

289

A spring moon so round
That my fingers are itching
   To touch its sharp edge.

290

A freezing morning:
As sharp as an aching tooth,
   A long icicle.

291

A wailing siren
Scales up sheer skyscraper walls
   In a blinding sun.

292

This tiny pimple,
So sunny bright on my cheek,
   Is bigger than I am.

293

As the bank teller
Jiggles a stack of silver,
  I think of sparrows.

294

The sound of a rat
Scampering over cold tin
  Is heard in the bowels.

295

A fly crawls slowly
Over a sticky paper,—
  How chilly the dawn!

296

Even my own shoes
Seem to become heavier
  This warm spring morning.

297

A chill autumn wind
Filling all the valley
    With mountain voices.

298

The sound of a snake
Slithering over dry leaves
    Is as hot as fire.

299

A descending fog
Is making an autumn day
    Taste of buried years.

300

On awakening,
I feel a cool autumn breeze
    Blowing on my brow.

301

A spring sky so clear
That you feel you are seeing
Into tomorrow.

302

There is where I am:—
Summer sunset loneliness,
Purple meeting red.

303

A balmy spring wind
Reminding me of something
I cannot recall.

304

Lonelier than dew
On shriveled magnolias
Burnt black by the sun.

305

This still afternoon
Is full of autumn sunlight
And spring memories.

306

Dazzling summer sun!
But the smell of the past comes
With rain upon the dust.

307

I feel autumn rain
Trying to explain something
I do not want to know.

308

A sleepless spring night:
Yearning for what I never had,
And for what never was.

309

She said she would come!
How yellow are these lilies!
How white is this sand!

310

Rotting yellow leaves
Have about them an odor
Both of death and hope.

311

The spring rain has blown
A shining little village
Upon a hillside.

312

How melancholy
That these sweet magnolias
Cannot smell themselves.

313

One, two, three stars
Breed a whole sky of stars,
   Dyeing the night blue.

314

Rustling dry paper
Sounding in an empty room
   Is a cold mountain.

315

In the setting sun,
Yellow roses are waving
   All their sharp wan thorns.

316

In the silent forest
A woodpecker hammers at
   The sound of silence.

317

Shrilling sparrows
Are sheathing the waterfall
With glittering light.

318

The fog's density
Deepens the croak of the frogs
On an April dawn.

319

How lonely it is:
A winter world full of rain,
Rain raining on rain.

320

A bay full of ships,
All arriving or leaving
On bright spring waves.

321

The ocean's soft sound
Lifts the toll of a far bell
To the half-seen stars.

322

Blowing from the sky,
And being blown toward the sky,—
Wild snow in April.

323

How lonely it is:
Black brittle cornstalks are snapping
In the winter blast.

324

Only one faint star,
One yellow-windowed ship
And one heaving sea.

325

Streaming on the hills,
Swirling past the horns of cows,
Steeply slanting snow.

326

Spring rain from the south,
And then spring rain from the north,—
How the green corn glistens!

327

Just enough of wind
To sway all the forest trees
In winter harmony.

328

The round horizon
Is black save for a red ball
In the cold mountains.

329

A little dog barks
At a roaring waterfall
    That swallows his voice.

330

White as it is young
And as black as it is dead, —
    One magnolia!

331

With her beak open,
A fat white hen is panting
    In the August heat.

332

While mounting a cow,
A bull ejaculates sperm
    On apple blossoms.

333

The neighing horses
Are causing echoing neighs
In neighboring barns.

334

A lakeshore circus:
An elephant trumpeting
Waves on blue water.

335

In an ice-wagon,
A snow-white pigeon sipping
Drops of cold water.

336

Hidden by snowflakes,
A horse neighs excitedly
In a white silence.

337

Blue-black beak open,
The crow hurls a caw straight at
A sinking red sun.

338

Tongue and tail drooping,
The dog trots in the noon-day sun,
Looking at nobody.

339

A cathedral bell
Dimming the river water
In the autumn dusk.

340

A bounding puppy
Chases a blue soap bubble
And barks when it bursts.

The indentation
Made by her head on the pillow:
A heavy snowfall.

A sinking red sun
Staining a snowy village:
A cock crows softly.

In winter twilight
A cawing crow flies over
A rain-wet village.

Out of icy fog,
Advancing with its sharp horns,
A white-faced cow.

345

The sad sound of hymns
Flooding on to autumn fields
In hazy moonlight.

346

Throughout the spring night,
The intermittent hooting
Of an owl in the rain.

347

As the sun dies down,
Last night's dew is still sparkling
Upon the lilacs.

348

A September fog,
Mute upon the empty porch
Of an empty house.

349

A church bell at dusk:
The evening sun's slanting rays
Dying on my wall.

350

Through sifting snow.
The ghostly outline of ships
In the quiet harbor.

351

Under a low sky
A boy walking with a dog
In the spring rain.

352

Why do I listen
To each low of the cow
This still autumn night?

353

Ascending swallows
Winging to cottony nests
In warm red clouds.

354

Tossing pine trees
Lulling a village to sleep
In the winter dusk.

355

An Indian summer
Heaps itself in tons of gold
Over Nigger Town.

356

In the cathedral,
In a lance of rosy light,
Clouds of lazy flies.

357

Above a gray lake,
In skyscraper window panes,
A dying spring day.

358

From out of the thickets
The sounds of trickling water
Fill the hazy fields.

359

Subsiding spring waves
Continue their slow rhythm
In the swaying trees.

360

A pink afterglow.
Behind nodding sunflowers
And the smell of mint.

361

At slow intervals
The hospital's lights wink out
In the summer rain.

362

The drone of spring rain;
A lonely old woman strokes
The fur of her cat.

363

A little girl stares,
Dewy eyes round with wonder,
At morning glories.

364

Hurdy-gurdy sounds
Soften the glow of streetlamps
In the evening dusk.

365

The Christmas season:
A whore is painting her lips
Larger than they are.

366

A cow is licking,
With long slow strokes of her tongue,
Spring rain from her thigh.

367

An old blindman
Playing a black violin
Amid fallen leaves.

368

While she undresses,
A spring moon touches her breasts
For seven seconds.

369

A tall sunflower
And a grinning little boy
    With snaggled teeth.

370

The baby's hiccough
Dies down and the hum of flies
    Fills the sunny room.

371

A peg-legged man
Stumps about in the garden,
    Pruning the roses.

372

A dead green beetle
Bobbing on a flowing creek,
    Beaten by spring rain.

RICHARD WRIGHT

373

A hunchback carries
A big black umbrella
    In the falling snow.

374

Hands behind his back,
An old priest on the seashore
    In the autumn sun.

375

The first day of spring:
The servant wears her blonde hair
    In a new manner.

376

A newspaper boy
Shouts "Extra!" in the cool night:
    Spring wind flaps his coat.

377

In the winter dusk,
A thin girl leads a black cow
    By a dragging rope.

378

Upon crunching snow,
Childless mothers are searching
    For cash customers.

379

In a freezing haze
The lowing of distant cows
    Fogs the window panes.

380

In the sea-scented wind
A prostitute is laughing
    With moon-glinting teeth.

381

On the summer air,
Flowing like rich creamy milk,
The low of a cow.

382

A valley village
Lies in the grip of moonlight:
How lonely it is.

383

Softer than sound,
The moon-struck magnolias
On a still hot night.

384

A dim yellow light
Glowing in a misty dawn
Makes a village cold.

385

Squeezing his eyes shut,
The cat yawns as if about
To eat the spring world.

386

A lost cat mews
In the sunset fleeciness
Of a cotton field.

387

The low of a cow
Answers a train's long whistle
In the summer dusk.

388

Faint in summer haze,
The contours of green hills
Through clouds of flies.

RICHARD WRIGHT

389

An autumn sunset
Casting shadows of tombstones
Over mounds of graves.

390

The crowded harbor:
Soft lights are blazing at dawn
In a drizzling rain.

391

The moon is over
The horns of a pregnant cow
In the April dusk.

392

Through white cotton fields,
Lifting toward the sunset,
A golden river.

393

An owl in moonlight
Perches on a sagging fence
In a summer field.

394

From a far valley
Comes the faint bark of a dog
Over yellow leaves.

395

The stars are dredging
The bottom of the spring river
For bits of blue steel.

396

A Spanish village:
Flowers and gurgling water,—
How silent it is!

397

Below hot wires
Throbbing with urgent appeals,
　　Poppies are blooming.

398

The October wind
Has blown the moon to a bit
　　Of brittle brass.

399

In the autumn woods
Mules grind juice from sugar cane
　　Under heavy clouds.

400

Under swelling clouds
Cutlasses flash in the sun
　　Amid sugar cane.

401

A thin mangy dog
Curls up to sleep in the dust
Of a moonlit road.

402

In the summer storm
A window shade is flapping
In my neighbor's house.

403

A pregnant cat
Licking its fuzzy belly
In a warm drizzle.

404

Out of autumn leaves,
An owl spits an angry hoot
At a dull-red moon.

405

In a bar's doorway,
Wiping his mouth in spring wind,
Seeing nobody.

406

Over railroad ties,
Heat rushes from hot mountains
On an August day.

407

In a light spring rain
An old woman is spitting
Into a handkerchief.

408

A dead mouse floating
Atop a bucket of cream
In the dawn spring light.

409

An icy drizzle
Slowly solidifying
    All the city's ash piles.

410

In the falling snow
The thick wool of the sheep
    Gives off a faint vapor.

411

When the school bell sounds,
A momentary silence
    Falls upon the birds.

412

In this rented room
One more winter stands outside
    My dirty window pane.

413

Why does that peach tree,
Arrayed in its pink blossoms,
Stand so near the pond?

414

A dog barks sharply
From the frozen black timbers
Of a burnt down house.

415

In a drizzling rain,
In a flower shop's doorway,
A girl sells herself.

416

A shaggy brown dog
Squatting under winter trees,
Shitting in the rain.

417

From a farmhouse porch,
A girl calls into the dusk
    Over snowy fields.

418

Whitecaps on the bay:
A broken signboard banging
    In the April wind.

419

In a hot valley,
White cattle standing as still
    As their black shadows.

420

A single letter
Fluttering in the mailbox:—
    A gusty spring wind.

421

This tenement room
In which I sweat this August
Has one buzzing fly.

422

My cigarette glows
Without my lips touching it,—
A steady spring breeze.

423

Settling on the screen
Of the crowded movie house,
A white butterfly.

424

Bits of confetti
Spotting a black umbrella
In an April rain.

425

An empty sickbed:
An indented white pillow
In weak winter sun.

426

A farmer's daughter
Screams at a contrary cow
In the driving sleet.

427

While crows are cawing,
Poppies are dutifully
Deepening their red.

428

From a green hilltop,
One tolling cathedral bell
Tints the spring sky blue.

429

Naked black children
Chasing down an alleyway
After a gray cat.

430

Raindrops are tilting
Pink from magnolias
In the setting sun.

431

Eating a red apple,
A little girl stares dreamily
At the autumn sea.

432

A gust of spring wind
Lifts a girl's white straw hat;
It floats on the lake.

433

Across her freckled face
Flitting shadows of snowflakes
Make her blue eyes blink.

434

A cock crows for dawn
And then a neighing horse tells
Of spring in his blood.

435

Look, look, look!
These are all the violets
Left by last night's rain!

436

A nude fat woman
Stands over a kitchen stove,
Tasting applesauce.

437

Through an open door,
Ruffling the skirts of the dolls,
A wind from spring hills.

438

About the kitten,
Who sleeps in a round white ball,
Are yellow tulips.

439

A church bell at dusk:
The evening sun's slanting rays
Dying on my wall.

440

Enough of spring rain
On the gutted country road
To fill wagon ruts.

441

In the autumn dusk:
A faintly lighted window
And the smell of rain.

442

Over yellow corn,
As muted as the sunset,
The low of a cow.

443

Snowing on the lake,
Snowing on the limbs of elms,
Snowing on spring snow.

444

When the letter came,
The autumn sea sounded sad
And the clouds stood still.

445

A loud ticking clock
Sounds in rhythm with the heat
Of a long slow day.

446

Sleepy bumble bees
Buzzing about plum blossoms
In the setting sun.

447

An early dawn breeze
Blowing with slow tenderness
On tall sunflowers.

448

A washerwoman
Dyes a tub of water blue,—
The sunlit spring wind!

449

Announcing autumn,
One dry leaf taps with crisp sound
On my window pane.

450

In a barbershop
The stench of soap and hair,—
A hot summer day!

451

As though sleepwalking,
A gray cat crosses the sand
In yellow moonlight.

452

A black woman sings:
Filling the sunlight with steam,
Bubbling molasses.

453

The sound of a rat
Gnawing in the winter wall
Of a rented room.

454

Waving red banners
Are whipping the clouds along
In a wild spring rain.

455

The green cockleburs
Caught in the thick wooly hair
Of the black boy's head.

456

Is it possible
That those wildly cawing crows
Know it is sunset?

457

A railroad station:
A crowd of summer children
   Laughing in the rain.

458

A tall pretty girl
Wearing a purple raincoat
   In the month of June.

459

I am paying rent
For the lice in my cold room
   And the moonlight too.

460

Sunday's church bell tolls
On a bright green sloping hill
   Over grazing cows.

461

Entering my town
In a heavy fall of snow,
I feel a stranger.

462

A train roars past
The eternal green of fields
In a rush of steam.

463

Of generations
Comes this wild red rose to me,
As I come to it.

464

In a vast silence
A wooden gate is open
In a spring farmyard.

465

Your cargo tonight,
Is it rain or hail or sleet,
Caravan of clouds?

466

The sound of spring thunder,
As wide as the wet plain
Over which it rolls.

467

A radiant moon
Shining on flood refugees
Crowded on a hill.

468

I have lost my way
In a strange town at night, —
A sky of cold stars.

469

The spring flood waters
Lap slowly at the doorsteps,—
   A radiant moon.

470

As I stand stockstill,
A viper undulates past,
   Unaware of me.

471

Rushing to the gate
To give her her parasol:
   The dawn stars were bright.

472

Even the serpent,
Magically beautiful
   In silver moonlight.

473

Between today's snow
And that which fell yesterday,
A night of bright stars.

474

A white butterfly
Sits with slowly moving wings
On a dead black snake.

475

Walking home alone
From the sporting arena:
A curve of spring moon.

476

A rain-wet buzzard
Amid dripping magnolias
In the setting sun.

477

On a bayonet,
And beyond the barbs of wire,—
A spring moon at dawn.

478

Wisps of winter fog
Left by the streetsweeper's broom
Along the gutters.

479

Head bent in spring sun,
A dog whimpers now and then,
Licking his penis.

480

Bolting the gate tight
Against all the autumn world,
Save the fiery stars.

481

Shut in the ice box,
A cricket chirps sleepily
In an alien winter.

482

At a funeral,
Strands of filmy spider webs
On coffin flowers.

483

Does the snail know that
The green leaf on which it sleeps
Is obeying the wind?

484

The horse's hot piss
Scalds a fragile nest of ants
In a sea of foam.

485

After a great yawn,
The cat blinks his eyes and stares
Past the autumn sun.

486

Two flies locked in love
Were hit by a newspaper
And died together.

487

"What a huge snowflake!"
But as I spoke my hot breath
Made it disappear.

488

As a big cloud melts,
Smaller and whiter clouds appear
Deeper in the sky.

489

Standing in the field,
I hear the whispering of
    Snowflake to snowflake.

490

Waking from a nap
And hearing summer rain falling,—
    What else has happened?

491

How lonely it is:
A ram unskins his penis,
    Shows the moon his teeth.

492

When I turn about,
My shadow lies alongside
    That of a scarecrow.

493

Wetting everything,
Wafting unseen and unheard,
Misty winter rain.

494

Turning a corner,
I duck my head to dodge
A new winter moon.

495

Through the church window,
Into the holy water,
A dry leaf flutters.

496

Sowing turnip seed
And glancing up and seeing
That the sun has gone.

497

A cool April breeze
Clears out the smoke of incense
From the cathedral.

498

How lonely it is:
The snowstorm has made the world
The size of my yard.

499

Just one lonely road
Stretching into the shadows
Of a summer night.

500

The sport stadium:
Every seat is taken
By whirling snowflakes.

501

Autumn moonlight is
Deepening the emptiness
Of a country road.

502

While the village sleeps,
The autumn stars come and fade,
Leaving a thin mist.

503

A long empty road
Under a lowering sky
In a winter dawn.

504

Across the table cloth,
Ants are dragging a dead fly
In the evening sun.

505

An empty canoe
Turning slowly on a river
In the autumn rain.

506

Pathetically,
A moth haunts a moonlit patch
Of white-plastered wall.

507

From out of nowhere,
A bird perches on a post,
And becomes a crow.

508

It is September,
The month in which I was born;
And I have no thoughts.

509

Tell me, Tin Soldier,
Of the spring daydreams you had
And never told me!

510

With its first blossom,
The little apple tree brags:
"Look, look! Me too!"

511

The fire in the grate
Lights up six dead soldiers,
And five standing.

512

If pumpkins could talk,
I am sure that they would be
Reactionary!

513

A toy railroad train
Stalled in a dusty station
   By webs of spiders.

514

"Say, Mr. Beetle,
Are you taking a detour
   Crawling on my knee?"

515

An old winter oak:
Once upon a time there was
   A big black ogre . . .

516

The lighted toy shop
Seen through a frozen window
   Is another world.

517

Like a big black giant
The child's shadow grimaces
On the moonlit wall!

518

Creamy plum blossoms:
Once upon a time there was
A pretty princess . . .

519

Even my old friends
Seem like newly met strangers
In this first snowfall.

520

O if I could live
In that house where a peach tree
Blooms in the rain!

521

Just enough of snow
To make you look carefully
At familiar streets.

522

My binoculars
Show me far across the bay,
Narcissus flowers.

523

Just enough of snow
To make a strutting black cock
Unbelievable.

524

A green postage stamp:
Blooming in an exotic land,
A far-away spring.

525

Only the horses
Really know the exact hour
When snow fell last night.

526

The arriving train
All decorated with snow
From another town.

527

Would not green peppers
Make strangely lovely insects
If they sprouted legs?

528

In the setting sun,
Red leaves upon yellow sand
And a silent sea.

529

Fire-fly, why play here?
The boys and girls are in the backyard,
Waiting for you.

530

My shadow was sad
When I took it from the sand
Of the gleaming beach.

531

O dark green melons,
Who shines your slick skins so smooth,
Making them mirrors?

532

As my delegate,
My shadow imitates me
This first day of spring.

533

What do they tell you
Each night, O winter moon,
    Before they roll you out?

534

A winter tempest
Has blown all the cloud stuffings
    Right out of the moon.

535

Has the day been long,
Morning, noon, and the cold night,
    O open-eyed dolls?

536

What did the moon hit
To make all those blue-green sparks
    Shower in the sky?

537

As silent as the snow
Sleeping in the cold moonlight
Of winter mountains.

538

What giant spider spun
That gleaming web of fire-escapes
On wet tenements?

539

Putting out the light,
The sound of the sleet hums sharper
Upon the tin roof.

540

As dark spring clouds sag,
The white buildings on the beach
Seem to come closer.

541

After the sermon,
The preacher's voice is still heard
In the caws of crows.

542

The dazzling spring sun
Dwindles the glittering sea
And shrinks the ships.

543

"Let's make a scarecrow!"
But after we had made it,
Our field grew smaller.

544

The spring sun has set;
The lake in its loneliness
Draws near the mountain.

545

The moon has gone down,
But its gleam is lingering
    On magnolias.

546

The sudden sunrise
Made the blooming apple tree
    Distant and smaller.

547

A layer of snow
Is pulling the mountains nearer,
    Making them smaller.

548

One caw of a crow
Tints all of the fallen leaves
    A deeper yellow.

549

A fluff of cotton
Floats up and is swallowed
By a vast white cloud.

550

Summer mountains move
To let a sinking sun pass
To the other side.

551

A black mountain peak
Is arching a summer sky
And its just-felt moon.

552

A small spring island
Is being measured by a
Ribbon of ship smoke.

553

Dazzling moonlight:
The shadows are as solid
As the dewy leaves.

554

The summer rainstorm
Drenches chickens in the fields,
Making them smaller.

555

So cold it is now
That the moon is frozen fast
To a pine tree limb.

556

The big light in the fog
Was but a little lantern
When we came to it.

557

The gale of autumn
Swept the trees clean of leaves
And drew the hills near.

558

Gleaming yellow pears
Were never so translucent
As in this scant rain.

559

Is this tiny pond
The great big lake in which
I swam as a boy?

560

For seven seconds
The steam from the train whistle
Blew out the spring moon.

561

An old lonely man
Had a long conversation
    Late one winter night.

562

A winter tempest
Is hurling the black-limbed trees
    Swiftly past the moon.

563

Could this melody
Be sung in other countries
    By other birds?

564

A hesitating sun
Turns a slow deep red and then
    Falls into the wheat.

565

A slow autumn rain:
The sad eyes of my mother
Fill a lonely night.

566

Into the dim room
A butterfly flits and flees, —
But can still be seen.

567

Bedraggled scarecrow,
What a time you must have had
In last night's rainstorm!

568

It is not outdoors
That the baby sparrow cheeps,
But here in the house!

569

A thin waterfall
Dribbles the whole autumn night,—
    How lonely it is.

570

For what does she wait,
Huddled in the winter rain,
    That young girl out there?

571

From across the lake,
Past the black winter trees,
    Faint sounds of a flute.

572

What will these moths do
When the bright streetlamps wink out
    And summer rain falls?

573

Twisting violently,
A lost kite seeks its freedom
From telegraph wires.

574

Standing in the crowd
In a cold drizzling rain,—
How lonely it is.

575

Between wagon shafts,
A horse waits in a cold rain
With its head hung low.

576

Calling and calling,
The faint voice of a sparrow
From the autumn rain.

577

Scarecrow, who starved you,
Set you in that icy wind,
And then forgot you?

578

In winter moonlight:
An empty railroad station
And one whining cat.

579

Amid the daisies
Even the idiot boy
Has a dignity.

580

My cold and damp feet
Feel as distant as the moon
On this autumn night.

581

Don't they make you sad,
Those wild geese winging southward,
O lonely scarecrow?

582

A limping sparrow
Leaves on a white window sill
Lacy tracks of blood.

583

A long winter rain:
A whistling old man whittles
A dream on a stick.

584

From the rainy dark
Comes faint white cries of wild geese,—
How lonely it is.

585

Suddenly one spring
She did not skip any more,
And her eyes grew grave.

586

Under plum blossoms,
Just castrated rams have tears
Bulging in their eyes.

587

In a damp attic,
Spilling out grains of sawdust,
A wounded rag doll.

588

For six dark dank years,
A doll with a Christmas smile
In an old shoe box.

589

From the cattle truck,
An anxious cow is staring
At springtime streets.

590

An old consumptive
Coughs so spasmodically
He disturbs the birds.

591

A sick cat seeks out
A stiff and frozen willow
Under which to die.

592

Sitting in spring rain,
Two forgotten rag dolls,
Their feet in water.

593

Lighting on my fence,
The crow tosses me a glance,
    Wipes his beak and goes.

594

O Cat with Gray Eyes,
Do you feel this autumn too,
    Are you also sad?

595

Two white butterflies
Fluttering over green grass:
    One goes east, one west.

596

A blue butterfly
Dips over a prison wall,
    Then slowly returns.

597

A slow encircling,
Inquisitive butterfly
   Follows the blindman.

598

The blindman stumbles,
Pauses, then walks slower
   Into the autumn night.

599

She has departed:
All the globes of golden pears
   Are pointed in pain.

600

Crying out the end
Of a long summer's sun,—
   Departing wild geese.

601

The train that took her
Steams into the autumn hills
And becomes silent.

602

A slow creeping snail;
Moments later I could not
See it anywhere.

603

The sound of a train
Fading in the autumn hills,—
And tomorrow too.

604

Departing wild geese
Are fanning the moon brighter
With their tireless wings.

605

Her train has now gone:
Where handkerchiefs were waving,
Moonlight on hot rails.

606

I last saw her face
Under a dripping willow
In a windy rain.

607

A cold winter sea
Blowing the hazy dawn stars
Higher and paler.

608

One vanishing ship
On an autumn horizon:
How lonely it is.

609

Black men with big brooms
Sweeping streets in falling snow,
Are absorbed by flakes.

610

In the blazing sun
The sand rose from the desert
And fled with the wind.

611

As the popcorn man
Is closing up his wagon,
Snow begins to fall.

612

Above leafless trees,
A crow skims a dark brown hill
And heads for the sun.

613

While plucking the goose,
A feather flew wildly off
  To look for snowflakes.

614

Like the day also,
Clouds are blown behind the hills
  By a winter wind.

615

Their watching faces,
As I walk the autumn road,
  Make me a traveler.

616

The snowball I threw
Was caught in a net of flakes
  And wafted away.

617

Starting a journey—
The scent of burning dry leaves
   Stains the sky lonely.

618

High above the ship
On which immigrants sail,
   Are departing geese.

619

As you leave the gate,
A skinny old dog barks once,
   Then goes back to sleep.

620

In the post office,
A clerk sorting out letters
   Hears spring rain falling.

621

A fleeing viper
Rippling rows of gold tassels
In a field of wheat.

622

Pen me a letter
From where plum trees are blooming,
Pilgrimaging geese!

623

Through the winter rain,
Calling to the scattered ships,
One floating sea gull.

624

Running here and there,
Twisting down the winter stream,
A tiny red shoe.

625

The caw of a crow:
On a distant summer field
Goes a silent train.

626

Off the cherry tree,
One twig and its red blossom
Flies into the sun.

627

As early as June,
One yellow leaf flutters down,
Calling to its brothers.

628

One umbrella
Entering into the woods
In a cold rain.

629

An autumn fog stares
At a cat in a doorway,
   Then steals slowly on.

630

For each baptized,
The brown creek laughs and gurgles,
   Flowing on its way.

631

In a winter dawn,
Fleeing an opening door,
   A scampering rat.

632

In the rainy dark
A train screams at each village,
   Then rolls on to the next.

633

A steamboat's whistle
Was blasted by the spring wind
To another town.

634

Over gleaming snow,
Lashing the moon on its way,
One swaying treetop.

635

An empty seashore:
Taking a long summer with it,
A departing train.

636

How lonely it is:
A rattling freight train has left
Fields of croaking frogs.

637

Was it a young man
Who went into the graveyard
In the summer rain?

638

In my sleep at night,
I keep pounding an anvil
Heard during the day.

639

And also tonight,
The same evening star above
The same apple tree.

640

The spring hills grow dim,
Today joining other days,
Days gone, days to come.

641

Another day falls
Out of a rainy curtain
Of dark autumn days.

642

It is as it is:
Yesterday's spring rain falling
All night and today.

643

In the autumn air,
Distant mountains are dreaming
Of autumns to come.

644

How many autumns
Has this giant rock been host to
The moon and its light?

645

From the mountain peak,
Crystal clear in summer air,
Winter without end.

646

This night too is night,
Night in a full net of nights
Made of autumn days.

647

Burning out its time,
And timing its own burning,
One lonely candle.

648

I am positive
That this is the same spring wind
That I felt yesterday.

649

Breathless and weary,
The fog lays its huge white head
On cherry blossoms.

650

How could this rose die?
This rich red color perish?
This sweet odor fade?

651

On a spring evening,
Clumsy clouds are teasing a moon
Too sleepy to care.

652

The leaves and the rain
Are whispering hurriedly
Under growling skies.

653

You can see the wind
Absentmindedly fumbling
With apple blossoms.

654

Defending themselves,
The green leaves beat back the rain,
Smashing it to mist.

655

With nervous pleasure,
The tulips are receiving
A spring rain at dusk.

656

The storm singles out
The tallest pine in the woods
And flays its branches.

657

Under the first snow
Yellow leaves are surrendering
With faint dry whispers.

658

The naked mountains,
Washing themselves in spring rain
As green fields look on.

659

The spring dawn comes so fast
That the yellow streetlamps
Turn pale and grow shy.

660

Between night and dawn,
A plum tree apologized
With profuse petals.

661

The lake gulps spring rain,
Sucking the falling drops
    With a million mouths.

662

I wonder how long
Was that violet dancing
    Before I saw it?

663

In the autumn dusk
A spider patiently darns
    A hole in a wall.

664

In the summer dawn,
Before it has time to dress,
    How sad the willow.

665

Winter wind brings snow
And gives the cat a litter
Of spotted kittens.

666

Golden afternoon:
Tree leaves are visiting me
In their yellow clothes.

667

That sparrow bent down,
Its head tucked beneath its wing,—
Sewing a button?

668

It is so hot that
The scarecrow has taken off
All his underwear!

669

A leaf chases wind
Across an autumn river
   And shakes a pine tree.

670

Accidentally
Cut by the tip of the hoe,
   The scarecrow shudders.

671

A pale winter moon,
Pitying a lonely doll,
   Lent it a shadow.

672

When the horse whinnies,
The scarecrow waves both his arms,
   Asking for silence.

673

A flood of spring rain
Searching into drying grasses
Finds a lost doll.

674

How it is bristling
Toward that big brassy sun,
This one sunflower.

675

In rippling water
A short black broomstick handle
Is a runaway snake.

676

After a meeting
Held in the corner garden,
The leaves scattered.

677

A skinny scarecrow
And its skinnier shadow
Fleeing a cold moon.

678

Turning here, there,
Leaping before sleety wind,
A lost yellow fan.

679

Suddenly mindful,
The tree was looking at me,
Each green leaf alive.

680

That fog standing there,
Inspecting the store window,
Is white with envy.

681

"Come out of the cold!"
A lighted window beckons
Through falling snow.

682

August noon hour:
All the objects of the world
Digesting shadows.

683

The cold is so sharp
That the shadow of the house
Bites into the snow.

684

As my delegate,
The scarecrow looks pensively
Into spring moonlight.

685

Jagged icicles
Are snapping off as they bite
Into the morning sun.

686

A darting sparrow
Startles a skinny scarecrow
Back to watchfulness.

687

Each moment or two
A long tongue of autumn wind
Licks the river white.

688

The autumn river
Utters one long crow cry,
Then rustles again.

689

His task completed,
The scarecrow watches the truck
Leave loaded with corn.

690

And now once again
Winter wind breathes sighingly
Amid the pine trees.

691

Made stiff by the sleet,
The flag stands out from the pole,
Like a general.

692

The ocean in June:
Inhaling and exhaling,
But never speaking.

693

One sad, one shy,
Low on the spring horizon,
    The sun and the moon.

694

It was so silent
That the silence protested
    With one lone bird cry.

695

My decrepit barn
Sags full of self-consciousness
    In this autumn sun.

696

Having appointed
All the stars to their places,
    The summer wind sleeps.

697

Smoking brick chimneys
Belching up a misshapen moon
In an autumn haze.

698

Black winter hills
Nibbling at the sinking sun
With stark stumpy teeth.

699

Flitting through the trees,
Some snowflakes cling to the twigs,
Others flutter free.

700

A dark forest plain
Is eagerly swallowing
Its first winter snow.

701

The sticky snowflakes
Cling stubbornly to the broom
Brushing them away.

702

The pennants are down,
But their black poles are boasting
To the snowy fields.

703

In tense dry panic,
A fallen leaf goes flying
Over other leaves.

704

The scarecrow's big sleeves
Advertising in the sun:
Huge, red tomatoes!

705

On a scarecrow's head,
A sparrow braces itself
   Against the spring wind.

706

Chattering dryly,
Yellow leaves are fleeing,
   Huddling in corners.

707

A shower of hail
Has beaten the spring moon thin
   And flattened the lake.

708

A wild winter wind
Is tearing itself to shreds
   On barbed-wire fences.

709

With the forest trees cut,
The lake lies naked and lost
In the bare hills.

710

Light flakes of snow
Being driven from the sky
By one yellow rose.

711

With solemnity
The magpies are dissecting
A cat's dead body.

712

The clouds are smiling
At a single yellow kite
Swaying under them.

713

The creeping shadow
Of a gigantic oak tree
   Jumps over the wall.

714

He hesitated
Before hanging up his coat
   On the scarecrow's arm.

715

Before blossoming,
A cherry bud looks eager,
   As if about to speak.

716

With mouth gaping wide,
Swallowing strings of wild geese,—
   Hungry autumn moon.

RICHARD WRIGHT

717

Backing off slowly,
The dog barks at a spring moon,
Just to make certain.

718

While plowing the earth,
Hills that were invisible
Are now to be seen.

719

Crystal April air:
A distant crow's beak opens,
Then a lagging caw.

720

A wilting jonquil
Journeys to its destiny
In a shut bedroom.

721

As my anger ebbs,
The spring stars grow bright again
And the wind returns.

722

Lines of winter rain
Gleam only as they flash past
My lighted window.

723

In the afterglow
A snow-covered mountain peak
Sings of loneliness.

724

As the stores are closing,
Yellow streetlamps spring to life
In an April fog.

725

From a cotton field
To magnolia trees,
 A bridge of swallows.

726

In the April sun,
The top of a damp sand mound
 Is slowly sifting.

727

Hopping on the fence,
A sparrow casts its shadow
 On a horse's flank.

728

Beneath pale stars,
Breathing wet on cattle horns,
 A faint winter fog.

729

Each ebbing sea wave
Makes pebbles glare at the moon,
Then fall back to sleep.

730

From the cherry tree
To the roof of the red barn,
A cloud of sparrows flew.

731

Even while sleeping,
The scabby little puppy
Scratches his fleas.

732

In the summer rain
A spider clinging grimly
To a sunflower.

733

In a dank basement
A rotting sack of barley
   Swells with sprouting grain.

734

A magnolia
Fell amid fighting sparrows,
   Putting them to flight.

735

Just before sunrise,
And after the milkman has gone,
   A jonquil blooms.

736

In the July sun,
Three birds flew into a nest;
   Only two came out.

737

In the summer sun,
Near an empty whiskey bottle,
A sleeping serpent.

738

In the burning sun,
A viper's tongue is nudging
A cigarette butt.

739

Out of the forest
One bird cry comes over snow,
Then black silence.

740

Drying in the sun,
Gleaming in a dirt pathway,
The track of a snail.

741

In the vast desert,
The whisper of stirring sand
Deepens the silence.

742

The sun is drying
Yellow leaves stuck on the wall
By last night's rainstorm.

743

In the still orchard
A petal falls to the grass;
A bird stops singing.

744

Only where sunlight
Spots the table cloth with gold
Do the flies cluster.

In the summer lake,
The moon gives a long shiver,
Then swells round again.

746

Spring snow melting,
But under the dark hedges
Are patches of white.

747

A crow calls out twice,
Then after a long silence
Calls out twice again.

748

Three times a bird calls;
At last there comes a response,
Meek and far away.

749

From the woods at night
Comes the sound of something walking
Over fallen leaves.

750

The mailman's whistle
Makes the weeping baby pause
And stare waitingly.

751

During spring cleaning,
She comes across her old dolls
And stares musingly.

752

How quiet it is when
The rain stops and changes
Into driving snow.

753

I saw the dead man
Impatiently brush away
    The flies from his mouth.

754

While urinating,
I feel slightly self-conscious
    Before the spring moon.

755

A bloated dead cat
Emerging from melting snow
    On a tenement roof.

756

So insistently
A crow caws in the spring field
    That I want to look.

757

In a quiet forest,
Out of a pool of cold rain,
A rat laps the stars.

758

Damp with autumnness,
On a dusty mantelpiece,
A porcelain hen.

759

Like remembering,
The hills are dim and distant
In the winter air.

760

An autumn river:
A crow with a broken wing,
Cawing as it floats.

761

An autumn evening,
With all its somber joy,
Is a lonely thing.

762

Droning autumn rain:
A boy lines up toy soldiers
For a big battle.

763

Beyond a sea wall,
An occasional wave flings
Foam at the autumn sky.

764

The oaken coffin,
Between the porch and the car,
Was christened by snow.

765

On a glassy sea
There is not a single ship
In the August sun.

766

Standing in the snow,
A horse shifts his heavy haunch
Slowly to the right.

767

A moment ago
There was just one icy star
Above that mountain.

768

This well-thumbed novel
Was the tale she loved best,—
Fields of autumn rain.

769

The calliope fades,
But the autumn wind still echoes
Its tune in the street.

770

My guests have now gone;
The grate fire burns to white ashes,—
How lonely it is.

771

Waving pennants gone,
The white houses now belong
To a summer sky.

772

The autumn wind moans:
I would like to talk to her,
If she were here now.

773

The parade has gone:
A cloudy sky rests heavier
Upon the houses.

774

On my trouser leg
Are still a few strands of fur
From my long dead cat.

775

After the parade,
And after the pounding drums,
Winter trees are distant.

776

Empty autumn sky:
The bright circus tents have gone,
Taking their music.

777

The wild geese have gone;
The hills over which they flew
Are grieving and black.

778

Having sold his cows,
His wide green pasture becomes
A part of the world.

779

The descending fog
Wipes out the foreign freighters
Anchored in the bay.

780

The parade has gone,
But the pounding drums still sway
The magnolias.

781

There is nobody
To watch the kitten playing
With the willow tip.

782

From the dark still pines,
Not a breath of autumn wind
To ripple the lake.

783

I cannot find it,
That very first violet
Seen from my window.

784

In this dry orchard
There are no red ripe apples
Dripping with rain.

785

I see nobody
Upon the muddy roadway
    In autumn moonlight.

786

In the winter dusk,
No trees are dotting the banks
    Of the little river.

787

This autumn evening
Is full of an empty sky
    And one empty road.

788

Around the tree trunk,
A kitten's paw is flicking
    At an absent mouse.

789

In the spring hills,
My dog sits and stares at me,—
Just us two alone.

790

In winter twilight
A black rat creeps along
A path in the snow.

791

In deep deference
To the fluttering snowflakes,
The birds cheep softly.

792

Does that sparrow know
That it is upon my roof
That he is hopping?

793

Not even the cat
Could escape the sudden rain
From the July sky.

794

After the snowstorm,
The cattle stands aimlessly,
Blinking at whiteness.

795

A tolling church bell:
A rat rears in the moonlight
And stares at the steeple.

796

Escaping spring rain,
Scuttling over a door sill,
A fuzzy spider.

797

A freezing midnight:
An empty house creaks slightly,
Settling in the earth.

798

Above corn tassels
Half lost in the evening's haze,
A single frog's croak.

799

A caterpillar
Sleeping in his spotted skin
On a sunlit leaf.

800

From under the house
My cat comes with dusty fur
And cobwebbed whiskers.

801

In a full zinc tub,
Winter rain pelting a rat,
    Floating and bloated.

802

A cat is watching
The fog as it is rising
    Out of frozen grass.

803

That rotting plant
Must be something delicious
    To that butterfly.

804

The guard on duty
Sees all visitors except
    The beads of spring dew.

805

One crow on a limb;
Another goes to join him,
Then both fly away.

806

The plow-split anthill
Reveals scurrying black cities
Under the horse's tail.

807

It was the first time
I had ever seen the rain
Blow a bird away.

808

Moonlit stillness:
One sear leaf makes sixty fall
With a sighing hiss.

809

Why did this spring wood
Grow so silent when I came?
What was happening?

810

That frozen star *there*,
Or *this* one on the water, —
Which is more distant?

811

All the long spring day
Poplar trees flinging raindrops
Against sunlit clouds.

812

Blossoming purple,
A forgotten artichoke
In a dark cupboard.

813

A winter dawn breathes
Tiny beads of sweat on a
    Sooty oil-lamp globe.

814

Clutching from the trees,
Thick creepers are strangling clouds
    In the lake's bosom.

815

Glittering with frost,
A dead frog squats livingly
    In the garden path.

816

Heading toward the sea,
Drifting into the cold rain,—
    How strong the smoke is!

On a scaly oak,
In the glare of sunset rays,
Ice on eagle's wings.

NOTES ON THE HAIKU

1

This haiku first appeared in Ollie Harrington, "The Last Days of Richard Wright," *Ebony*, no. 16 (February 1961): 93. It also is included in *Richard Wright Reader*, eds. Ellen Wright and Michel Fabre (New York: Harper & Row, 1978), p. 253. In both versions the first line reads: "I am nobody" without a colon. For a critical commentary on the haiku, see Afterword.

2

This haiku first appeared in Richard Wright, "Fourteen Haikus," *Studies in Black Literature* 1 (Autumn 1970), 1. It also is included in *Richard Wright Reader*, p. 251, as the first one. Both versions read: "For you, O gulls / I order slaty waters / And this leaden sky."

In Wright's manuscript, an exclamation mark at the end of the third line may be a substitute for a *kireji* (cutting word). The classic *renga* (linked verse) had eighteen varieties of *kireji* for dividing its sections: *ya*, *kana*, *keri*, etc. Basho increased the variety to forty-eight as the use of *kireji* was re-defined and expanded. In "The Old Pond" the syllable *ya* is attached to the words *furu ike* (old pond): Basho is expressing a feeling of awe about the quietness of the pond. In another celebrated haiku, Basho uses *ya* to emphasize the deadly quiet atmosphere of the woods he visited: *"Shizukesa ya / Iwa ni shimi iru / Semi no koe"* (It's deadly quiet: / Piercing into the rocks / Is the shrill of cicada). Above all, adding a *kireji* is a structural device to "cut" or divide a whole into parts. Since composing a haiku is confined to seventeen syllables in three lines, the parts of a vision or idea must be clearly segmented and united in its development. Dividing the whole into its sections, in turn, gives the section with a *kireji* great weight. The use of cutting words in haiku thus signifies the poet's conviction about a natural phenomenon with which he or she is struck. Because the poet's response to the scene is interpreted as decisive, the overall vision created in the poem is further clarified. Traditionally, cutting words convey one's hope, wish, demand, call, question, resignation, awe, wonder, surprise, and the like.

3

This haiku first appeared in *Ebony*, no. 16 (February 1961): 93. It also is included in *Richard Wright Reader*, p. 253. Both versions delete the comma at the end of the first line and the period at the end of the third line. Wright might have used a comma as a substitute for a cutting word, as explained in note 2.

The third line constitutes a *kigo* (season word) referring to spring. The close tie haiku has to nature is manifested by making reference to one of the four seasons and appreciating its beauty. Conventionally, a letter in Japanese begins with a seasonal greeting and a reference to weather. This custom may have derived from the poets of the Muromachi period (1392–1573) who perceived the season in each climatic, environmental, and biological phenomenon—spring rain, winter snow, cherry blossoms, falling leaves, autumn sunset, the harvest moon, and the like—by which it became a literary representation. A seasonal word gives each haiku a vastness and universality it might not ordinarily have. This reference gives the poem a sense of infinity and eternity as it itself remains finite and temporary. In addition, the *kigo* serves an aesthetic function since it has a capacity to evoke commonly perceived images of beauty. Buson's "Yama Dori no" (The Mountain Pheasant) uses the spring setting sun for the *kigo: "Yama dori no / O mo fumu haru no / Iri hi kana"* (Also stepping on / The mountain pheasant's tail is / The spring setting sun). Seasonal words are often associated with certain conventional perceptions and implications. For example, morning glories evoke the thought of quickly fading beauty, autumn winds imply loneliness and sadness, and plum blossoms suggest that they are merely precursors of perfect beauty to be created by later cherry blossoms.

7

This haiku first appeared in *Ebony*, no. 16 (February 1961): 93. It also is included in *Richard Wright Reader*, p. 253. Both versions read: "Make up your mind snail! / You are half inside your house / And halfway out!" For a commentary, see Afterword.

13

This haiku first appeared in *Studies in Black Literature* 1 (Autumn 1970), 1. It also appeared in Richard Wright, "Haiku," *New Letters* 38 (Winter 1971), 101. It also is included in *Richard Wright Reader*, p. 251. Both versions omit a period in the third line. The haiku in its simple depiction of a spring scene is reminiscent of a well-known haiku by Buson:

Tsuri-gane ni	On the hanging bell
Tomarite nemuru	Has perched and is fast asleep,
Kocho kana	It's a butterfly.

17

A misty rain and a butterfly suggest spring. This haiku expresses the poet's perception of a harmony that exists among the insect, the animal, and their climatic environment.

18

In this description of a summer scene, the pavements— man-made objects—appear as a discordant element against the natural background: a sparrow, its excrement, and the summer heat.

20

This haiku first appeared in *Studies in Black Literature* 1 (Autumn 1970), 1. It also appeared in *New Letters* 38 (Winter 1971), 101. It also is included in *Richard Wright Reader,* p. 251. All three versions omit a period at the end of the poem.

21

Although this haiku describes an interaction between man and nature, as does Kikaku's famous haiku "The Harvest

Moon," the central image created in it represents a different kind of interaction, one between man and animal. The interaction in "The Harvest Moon" creates a far more luminous image than moonlight itself. For a further commentary on Kikaku's poem, see Afterword.

22

This haiku first appeared in *Ebony*, no. 16 (February 1961): 93. It also is included in *Richard Wright Reader*, p. 254. A period is lacking in both versions. For a critical commentary on the haiku, see Afterword.

25

A sense of incongruity that the courtyard, part of man's world, and the urination of a horse convey makes this verse a *senryu* rather than a haiku. The incongruity, however, seems to lie in the human perception rather than in the scene, as the situation is common. For *senryu*, see Afterword.

28

For a commentary, see Afterword.

31

This haiku first appeared in *Ebony*, no. 16 (February 1961): 93. It also is included in *Richard Wright Reader*, p. 253. A period is lacking in both versions. For a critical commentary on the haiku, see Afterword.

42

This piece finds unity in man and nature: a man, a mule, a rain, a meadow, and a hill.

45

Although the final line is in four syllables, it provides emphasis with an exclamation mark. This haiku expresses a perception that nature is intricate and infinite. For the syllabic convention in haiku, see Afterword.

47

This haiku first appeared in *Ebony*, no. 16 (February 1961): 93. It also is included in *Richard Wright Reader*, p. 254. Both versions omit a period at the end of the poem. For a critical commentary on the haiku, see Afterword.

50

For a commentary, see Afterword.

57

For a commentary, see Afterword.

62

For a commentary, see Afterword.

64

This haiku describes the arrival of spring with a transference of the senses: the scent of oranges and the warmth of March wind. The image of a harbor at dawn suggests the protection of man from the winter weather.

66

For a commentary, see Afterword.

69

This haiku first appeared in *Ebony*, no. 16 (February 1961): 94. It also is included in *Richard Wright Reader*, p. 254. In both versions, the first line does not have a comma after "leave," nor does the second line after "rain." For a critical commentary on the haiku, see Afterword.

83

This one, in a simple description of change and loss in nature, expresses a sense of *yugen* characteristic of classic Japanese haiku. For a discussion of *yugen*, see Afterword.

84

This is a haiku of balance and harmony: not only does a yellow butterfly, an image of beauty, counterbalance the pond's green scum, an image of ugliness, but the entire scene becomes beautiful because of two yellow butterflies, perhaps a couple, instead of one.

103

This haiku first appeared in *Studies in Black Literature* 1 (Autumn 1970), 1. It also appeared in *New Letters* 38 (Winter 1971), 100. It also is included in *Richard Wright Reader*, p. 252. In all three versions, a period is lacking at the end of the poem.

106

An image of nature, "beads of quicksilver," is reinforced by a man-made object, "a black umbrella," under a natural environment.

117

This haiku first appeared in *Ebony*, no. 16 (February 1961): 94. It also appeared in *New Letters* 38 (Winter 1971), 100. It also is included in *Richard Wright Reader*, p. 254. A period is lacking in all three versions. For a critical commentary on the haiku, see Afterword.

125

This one, with a vague reference to autumn, expresses a sense of loneliness as do many classic Japanese haiku. For a discussion of classic Japanese haiku, see Afterword.

135

Even though human beings try to take advantage of nature, it does not always let them. Nature has its autonomy.

136

This haiku describes a dark, desolate scene in autumn. Like Basho's haiku on autumn, it conveys a sensibility of *yugen* and *sabi*. For a discussion of *yugen* and *sabi*, see Afterword.

141

This haiku first appeared in *Studies in Black Literature* 1 (Autumn 1970), 1. It also is included in *Richard Wright Reader*, p. 251. Both versions read: "An autumn sunset / A buzzard sails slowly past / Not flapping its wings." For an expression of quietude and loneliness, it bears some resemblance to Basho's celebrated haiku "A Crow." For a discussion of Basho's poem, see Afterword.

142

For a critical commentary on this haiku, see Afterword.

143

This one first appeared in *Studies in Black Literature* 1 (Autumn 1970), 1. It also appeared in *New Letters* 38 (Winter 1971), 100. It also is included in *Richard Wright Reader*, p. 252. All three versions lack a question mark at the end and read: "Why is hail so wild / Bouncing so frighteningly / Only to lie so still."

145

For a commentary, see Afterword.

152

This haiku in an irregular measure of 5,6,4, and without a seasonal reference, sounds more like a modern haiku than a traditional one.

172

For a commentary, see Afterword.

173

This haiku depicts the arrival of spring with winter lingering over the mountains. Because of the bright sun, the beauty of snow is intensified; as a paradox, the poem extols winter while celebrating spring.

This one first appeared in *Studies in Black Literature* 1 (Autumn 1970), 1. It also is included in *Richard Wright Reader*, p. 251. A period is lacking in both versions. In describing one's poverty and isolation the haiku expresses the sensibility of *wabi*. For a discussion of *wabi*, see Afterword.

This haiku first appeared in *Studies in Black Literature* 1 (Autumn 1970), 1. It also appeared in *New Letters* 38 (Winter 1971), 100. It also is included in *Richard Wright Reader*, p. 252. A period is lacking in all three versions. For a critical commentary on the haiku, see Afterword.

This haiku first appeared in *Studies in Black Literature* 1 (Autumn 1970), 1. It also appeared in *New Letters* 38 (Winter 1971), 101. It also is included in *Richard Wright Reader*, p. 251. A period is lacking in all three versions.

185

In this haiku, a transference of the senses between the sound of the wind and the shape of drifting snow occurs.

194

A transference of the senses between the cracking of a tree limb and the starlight reflected on snow creates a beautiful image.

212

The convergence of the bustling streets into a spring sea suggests a harmony between humanity and nature.

220

The interaction between the bell and the spring moon reflected on the river suggests the unity of man and nature.

221

The scene arouses a tender feeling about nature: the mother duck's love and protection of her offspring and their obedience to and reliance upon her. "Even," placed at the beginning of the first line, functions as a cutting word and emphasizes the point of view. For more on the use of cutting words in haiku, see note 2.

224

This one expresses, as some contemporary Japanese haiku do, a sense of balance and harmony in human life. A feeling of happiness, suggested by the red roses, compensates for the loneliness suggested by convalescing, as the color of the flowers does for the absence of smell.

226

For a commentary, see Afterword.

230

A stark contrast between a lone cricket's cry and the serenity of the moon and stars, as well as an interaction of the senses between sight and sound, does create a sense of infinite space and silence.

239

There is a transference of the senses between the sound of an axe and the ripples on the lake.

241

The autumn fog, while keeping the living from seeing, creates beads of light, an image of beauty, for a man who unfortunately cannot see.

243

A feeling of isolation and loneliness, a modernist theme, is balanced by the presence of the doctor, just as night is by day and sadness by happiness.

264

This verse sounds more like a *senryu* than a haiku for an expression of humor and levity. For *senryu*, see Afterword.

265

A transference of the senses between the color and the sound of the sky makes the image of nature infinitely vast.

268

The first line, with two negative articles and a colon, functions as a *kireji* (cutting word). The coldness of the winter night is reinforced by a dog's barking whitely. For more on cutting words in haiku, see note 2.

276

This haiku depicts a transference between the smell of apples and the light of the moon.

292

This verse is a *senryu* rather than a haiku for an expression of light humor. For *senryu*, see Afterword.

As an expression of sympathy for a fly, this one is reminiscent of Issa's famous haiku "Do Not Ever Strike!": "Do not ever strike! / The fly moves as if to pray / With his hands and feet." In Issa's haiku, the negative particle attached to the verb "strike" functions as a cutting word. In Wright's haiku, the final line with "how" and an exclamation mark accomplishes the same effect. For a discussion of Issa's Buddhistic philosophy and his haiku, see Afterword. For cutting words in haiku, see note 2.

This haiku first appeared in Constance Webb, *Richard Wright: A Biography* (New York: G. P. Putnam's Sons, 1968), p. 393. It also appeared in *Studies in Black Literature* 1 (Autumn 1970), 1, and in *New Letters* 38 (Winter 1971), 100. It also is included in *Richard Wright Reader*, p. 253. Webb's version conforms to the manuscript but the other versions do not have a period at the end.

316

Describing the deep silence of the forest, this haiku is reminiscent of Basho's celebrated haiku "It's Deadly Quiet," quoted in note 2.

329

This verse is a *senryu* rather than a haiku. For *senryu*, see Afterword.

332

However spontaneously the scene is depicted, this verse sounds like a *senryu* rather than a haiku. For *senryu*, see Afterword.

365

This one gives a sensation similar to that of a modernist haiku by Yamaguchi Seishi: "Lo the Jupiter! / A prostitute was swimming / On the sea by day."

368

Since an erotic sensation expressed here is tempered by a reference to a spring moon, this haiku creates an image of fleeting beauty like that of cherry blossoms. In its subject matter, this piece smacks of modernist haiku.

377

It is not clear whether a girl leads a cow or a cow her: creating such an ambiguous image suggests the unity and harmony between man and nature.

380

In its subject matter this haiku, like 365, "The Christmas Season," is least traditional.

388

While this piece has an unusual 5,6,4 syllabic rhythm, it captures an aesthetic sensibility of *yugen*. For *yugen*, see Afterword.

401

For a critical commentary, see Afterword.

410

This piece has a 5,6,6 syllabic measure. The thick wool protecting the sheep from cold weather suggests a harmonious relationship between the animal and its natural environment.

412

Cast in a manner of *wabi*, this haiku focuses on the beauty of a winter scene in contrast to loneliness and poverty in human life. For a discussion of the aesthetic principle of *wabi*, see Afterword.

416

However spontaneous raining and shitting are, a sense of incongruity between the two natural phenomena makes this verse a *senryu*. For *senryu*, see Afterword.

Although this haiku describes nature's intrusion upon the human world, it suggests that the insect is perching on the screen as if it were flying in a natural scene projected on the screen.

This piece first appeared in *Studies in Black Literature* 1 (Autumn 1970), 1. It also appeared in *New Letters* 38 (Winter 1971), 101. It also is included in *Richard Wright Reader*, p. 252. In all three versions, a period is lacking at the end of the poem. For a critical commentary, see Afterword.

A transference of the senses between the tolling of the cathedral bell and the blue sky creates a harmonious picture of man and nature.

In its rhythm and subject matter, this piece resembles a modern haiku.

435

This piece has an unusual syllabic rhythm of 3,6,5. A repetition of the command "look" in the first line, with an exclamation mark, functions like a *kireji* in Japanese haiku. For *kireji*, see note 2.

444

The poet makes nature convey his sentiment, a manner that resembles T. S. Eliot's objective correlative.

455

This haiku first appeared in Constance Webb, *Richard Wright: A Biography*, p. 393. See note 303. It also appeared in *Studies in Black Literature* 1 (Autumn 1970), 1, and in *New Letters* 38 (Winter 1971), 101. It also is included in *Richard Wright Reader*, p. 253. Webb's version is identical with the manuscript version. The other versions do not have a period at the end of the poem. For a critical commentary on the haiku, see Afterword.

459

For an expression of *wabi*, this haiku focuses on the beauty of the moonlight in contrast to the lice. For a discussion of the sensibility of *wabi* and Rotsu the beggar-poet in seventeenth-century Japan, see Afterword.

467

As an expression of *wabi*, this haiku depicts the beauty of the moon and the affinity people have with their fellow human beings.

483

This verse expresses a typical haiku perception that all life belongs to nature.

484

In a coarse manner, this verse reads more like a *senryu* than a haiku. For *senryu*, see Afterword.

489

This haiku first appeared in Webb, *Richard Wright: A Biography*, p. 394. It also appeared in *Studies in Black Literature* 1 (Autumn 1970), 1. It also is included in *Richard Wright Reader*, p. 252. The versions in *Studies in Black Literature* and *Richard Wright Reader* both read: "Standing in the field / I hear the whispering of / Snowflake to snowflake." Webb's version is identical with the manuscript version, except that in Webb's the first line is not indented.

491

As an expression of *yugen* to portray loneliness, this haiku is essentially flawed. Not only is a ram's action graceless, but the entire scene fails to evoke a sense of mystery. The kind of incongruity and humor the poet tries to interject does not even make the verse a good *senryu*. For a discussion of *yugen*, see Afterword. For *senryu*, also see Afterword.

497

In depicting the spring atmosphere that permeates the cathedral, this is reminiscent of a modern Japanese haiku,

"From Hoojoo's," by Takano Suju: "From Hoojoo's / Huge and lofty temple roof: / Butterflies of spring."

508

This haiku first appeared in Webb's *Richard Wright: A Biography*, p. 394: "It is September / The month in which I was born, / And I have no thoughts." It also is included in *Richard Wright Reader*, p. 254: "It is September / The month when I was born / And I have no thoughts." Whether the *Richard Wright Reader* version is in error is not certain, but the manuscript version is in a usual syllabic measure of 5,7,5, whereas that of the *Richard Wright Reader* is in a 5,6,5 measure. For a critical commentary on the haiku, see Afterword.

535

This haiku without a seasonal reference and with slight humor sounds like a *senryu*. For seasonal references, see note 3. For *senryu*, see Afterword.

539

A transference of the senses between the light and the sound of the sleet intensifies the natural phenomenon.

Conceptually, this haiku reminds one that in contrast to nature, the human world is necessarily limited. Structurally, the poem thrives with the use of an exclamation mark in "cutting" the first line from the rest, as well as with the use of the comparative adjective "smaller" in the final line. For cutting words in haiku, see note 2.

569

For a perception of loneliness in autumn, this piece is reminiscent of Basho's famous haiku: "A crow / Perched on a withered tree / In the autumn evening." For a discussion of Basho's poem, see Afterword. For a commentary on this haiku by Wright, also see Afterword.

571

This one first appeared in *Studies in Black Literature* 1 (Autumn 1970), 1. It also is included in *Richard Wright Reader*, p. 252. Both versions read: "From across the lake / Past the black winter trees / Faint sounds of a flute." An interaction of nature and art occurs through a transference of the senses between the black winter trees and the faint sounds of a flute.

Both images, in turn, intensify each other. For further discussion of the haiku, see Afterword.

574

For a commentary, see Afterword.

577

For a commentary, see Afterword.

580

This one as an expression of pure sensation resembles one of Basho's lesser-known haiku: "How cool it is, / Putting the feet on the wall: / An afternoon nap." For a discussion of the haiku by Basho, see Afterword.

581

The middle line originates from a passage in *Black Boy:* "There were the echoes of nostalgia I heard in the crying strings of wild geese winging south against a bleak, autumn sky." See *Black Boy: A Record of Childhood and Youth* (New York: Harper, 1966 [1945]), p. 14.

584

Although this haiku is similar to 581, "Don't They Make You Sad," a transference of the senses occurs between the faint cries of wild geese and the whiteness of the birds against the rainy dark background.

600

For a commentary, see Afterword.

608

This haiku in a manner of *yugen* expresses the loneliness man feels in the wide world. For *yugen*, see Afterword.

626

This describes a scene in which a twig with its red blossom flies into the sun as if a bird flew off the cherry tree. In creating an illusion the poem is reminiscent of Moritake's famous haiku, which Ezra Pound quotes in his discussion of Japanese haiku: "The fallen blossom flies back to its branch: / A butterfly." For Pound's discussion of Moritake's haiku, see Ezra Pound, "Vorticism," *Fortnightly Review*, no. 573, n.s. (1914): 467; and Yoshinobu Hakutani, "Ezra Pound, Yone Noguchi, and Imagism," *Modern Philology* 90 (August 1992), 56.

647

This piece was first published in Webb, *Richard Wright: A Biography*, p. 400. According to Webb, Wright's daughter, Julia, while sitting with the haiku manuscript in her father's study after his death, wrote "This is Daddy," referring to the haiku. For a commentary on this haiku, see Afterword.

650

This haiku expresses in a manner of *yugen* that change constitutes one aspect of man and nature. For *yugen*, see Afterword.

657

This haiku in a manner of *yugen* expresses a perception that inevitable change takes place in nature. For a discussion of *yugen*, see Afterword.

660

For a commentary, see Afterword.

661

This one is in an unusual measure of 5,6,6 syllables.

668

Light humor makes this verse an excellent *senryu*. For *senryu*, see Afterword.

669

An illusion created in this haiku is akin to that in the classic haiku by Moritake, "The Fallen Blossom." For a discussion of Moritake's poem, see note on Wright's haiku 626, "Off the Cherry Tree." Wright's "A Leaf Chases Wind" is also similar to his other haiku, such as 627, "As Early As June," and 629, "An Autumn Fog Stares."

671

While the second line alludes to man's loneliness, a pale winter moon, natural beauty, is intensified by the presence of a manmade object. In this respect, the haiku bears some resemblance to Kikaku's "The Harvest Moon." For a discussion of Kikaku's haiku, see Afterword.

684

For a commentary, see Afterword.

695

In a manner of *wabi*, this haiku describes a contrast between man's poverty and nature's grandeur.

698

For a commentary, see Afterword.

709

This piece, in an unusual 6,7,4 syllabic rhythm, depicts a distortion of natural beauty brought about by man's exploitation of nature.

720

For a commentary, see Afterword.

721

Describing control of emotion, this haiku alludes to a state of mind called *mu* in Zen. For a discussion of Zen philosophy that underlies much of the classic Japanese haiku, see Afterword.

Only when an interaction between man and nature occurs can natural beauty be appreciated. For a further commentary, see Afterword.

723

For a commentary, see Afterword.

735

This haiku, in an unusual 5,8,4 syllabic measure, depicts a beautiful natural phenomenon without human intervention.

741

For a description of serenity in nature, this and 739, "Out of the Forest," resemble Basho's famous haiku "It's Deadly Quiet," quoted in note 2.

754

Because urinating and the spring moon are both natural phenomena, the scene of incongruity described makes this verse an excellent *senryu*. For *senryu*, see Afterword.

759

For a commentary, see Afterword. In a style of *yugen*, this haiku expresses an affinity between man and nature. For the poetic sensibility of *yugen*, see Afterword.

769

The term "calliope," which is also the name for the most important of the ancient Greek muses, here refers to the musical instrument with air or steam whistles used in carnivals, circuses, and on river boats. The reference plays the role of an intermediary between nature and art.

781

In a style of *wabi*, this poem expresses a feeling of isolation and loneliness: only the poet can appreciate such a beautiful play of the cat. For *wabi*, see Afterword.

783

For a commentary, see Afterword.

785

For an expression of *wabi*, this one is similar to 781, "There Is Nobody," above. For *wabi*, see Afterword.

787

With the use of a paradoxical word, "full," this piece conveys the sensibility of *wabi*. For *wabi*, see Afterword.

798

A single frog's croak intensifying a scene of mystery and nebulosity, this haiku is composed in a style of *yugen*. Traditionally, a frog is a seasonal reference to spring, but Yone Noguchi, a Japanese bilingual poet and critic, regarded Basho's famous haiku on a frog, "The Old Pond," as an autumn haiku. For Noguchi's discussion of Basho's haiku, see Yoshinobu Hakutani, ed., *Selected English Writings of Yone Noguchi: An East-West Literary Assimilation*

(Cranbury, N.J.: Associated University Presses, 1992), Vol. II, pp. 73–74.

803

A transference of the senses, especially among the sight of the butterfly, the smell, and the taste of the rotting plant occurring, this haiku is reminiscent of 47, "The Spring Lingers On."

808

For a depiction of nature's serenity, this haiku bears some resemblance to Basho's "It's Deadly Quiet," quoted in note 2.

809

This haiku seems inspired by Zen philosophy. For a discussion of haiku and Zen, see Afterword. For a further commentary on this haiku, also see Afterword.

AFTERWORD

I

Like transcendentalists such as Emerson and Whitman, Japanese haiku poets were inspired by nature, especially its beautiful scenes and seasonal changes.[1] Although the exact origin of haiku is not clear, the close relationship haiku has with nature suggests the ways in which the ancient Japanese lived on their islands. Where they came from is unknown, but they must have adapted their living to ways of nature. Many were farmers, others hunters, fishermen, and warriors. While they often confronted nature, they always tried to live in harmony with it: Buddhism and Shintoism taught them that the soul existed in them as well as in nature, the animate and the inanimate alike, and that nature must be preserved as much as possible.

Interestingly, haiku traditionally avoided such subjects as earthquakes, floods, illnesses, and eroticism—ugly aspects of nature. Instead, haiku poets were attracted to such objects as flowers, trees, birds, sunset, the moon, genuine love. Those who earned their livelihood by labor had to battle with the negative aspects of nature, but noblemen, priests, writers, singers, and artists found beauty and pleasure in natural phenomena. They had the time to idealize or romanticize nature and impose a philosophy on it, and as a result they became an elite group in Japanese culture. Basho was an essayist, Buson a painter, and Issa a Buddhist priest—and each was an accomplished haiku poet.

The genesis of haiku can be seen in the *waka* (Japanese song), the oldest verse form, of thirty-one syllables in five lines (5,7,5,7,7). As an amusement at court someone would compose the first three lines of a *waka* and another person would be challenged to provide the last two lines to complete the verse. The haiku form, a verse of seventeen syllables arranged 5,7,5, with such exceptions as 5,7,6 and 5,8,5, etc., corresponds to the first three lines of the *waka*. *Hyakunin Isshu* (*One Hundred Poems by One Hundred Poets*, A.D. 1235), a *waka* anthology compiled by Fujiwara no Sadaiye, contains haiku-like verses. Sadaiye's "Chiru Hana wo" ("The Falling Blossoms"), for example, reads:

Chiru hana wo	The falling blossoms:
Oikakete yuku	Look at them, it is the storm
Arashi kana[2]	That is chasing them.

The focus of this verse is the poet's observation of a natural object, the falling blossoms. To this beautiful picture Sadaiye adds his feeling about the phenomenon: it looks as though a storm is pursuing the falling flower petals.

This seventeen-syllable verse form was preserved by noblemen, courtiers, and high-ranked samurai for nearly three centuries after the publication of *Hyakunin Isshu*. Around the beginning of the sixteenth century, the verse form became popular among the poets. It constituted a dominant element of another popular verse form called *renga*, linked song. *Renga* was a continuous chain of fourteen (7,7) and seventeen (5,7,5) syllable verses, each independently composed, but connected as one poem. The first collection of *renga*, *Chikuba Kyojin Shu* (*Chikuba Mad Men's Collection*) contains over two hundred *tsukeku* (adding verses) linked with the first verses of another poet. As the title of this collection suggests, the salient characteristic of *renga* was a display of ingenuity and coarse humor. *Chikuba Kyojin Shu* also collected twenty hokku (starting verses). Because the hokku, which was an earlier term for haiku, was considered the most important verse of a *renga* series, it was usually composed by the senior poet attending a *renga* session. The fact that this collection included far fewer hokku in proportion to *tsukeku* indicates the poets' interest in the comic nature of the *renga*.[3]

By the 1680s, when Matsuo Basho (1644–1694) wrote the first version of his celebrated poem on the frog jumping into the old pond, an older poetic genre from which haiku evolved, *haikai*, had become a highly stylized expression of poetic vision.[4] Basho's poem was totally different from most of the *haikai* poems written by his predecessors: it was the creation of a new perception and not merely an ingenious play on words. As most scholars observe, the changes and innovations brought about in *haikai* poetry were not accomplished by a single poet.[5] Basho's contemporaries, with Basho as their leader, attempted to create the serious *haikai*, a verse form known in modern times as haiku. The haiku, then, was a unique poetic genre in the late seventeenth century that was short but could give more than wit or humor: a haiku became a crystallized expression of the poet's vision and sensibility.

To explain Basho's art of haiku, Yone Noguchi, a noted bilingual poet and critic, once quoted "Furu Ike ya" ("The Old Pond"):

Furu ike ya	The old pond!
Kawazu tobi komu	A frog leapt into—
Mizu no oto[6]	List, the water sound!

One may think a frog an absurd poetic subject, but Basho focused his vision on a scene of desolation, an image of nature. The pond was perhaps situated on the premises of an ancient temple whose silence was suddenly broken by a frog plunging into the deep water. As Noguchi conceived the experience, Basho, a Zen Buddhist, was "supposed to awaken into enlightenment now when he heard the voice bursting out of voicelessness."[7] According to Noguchi, Basho realized at the moment of enlightenment that life and death were merely different aspects of the very same thing. Basho was not suggesting that the tranquillity of the pond meant death or that the frog symbolized life. Basho here had the sensation of hearing the sound bursting out of soundlessness. A haiku is not a representation of goodness, truth, or beauty; there is nothing particularly good, true, or beautiful about a frog's leaping into the water.

It seems as though Basho, in writing the poem, carried nature within him and brought himself to the deepest level of nature, where all sounds lapse into the world of silence and infinity. Though his vision is based upon reality, it transcends time and space. What a Zen poet like Basho is showing is that man respects nature, appreciates it, and achieves his peace of mind. This fusion of man and nature is called "spontaneity" in Zen. The best haiku, because of their linguistic limitations, are inwardly extensive and outwardly infinite. A severe constraint imposed on one aspect of haiku must be balanced by a spontaneous, boundless freedom on the other.

From a Zen point of view, such a vision is devoid of intellectualism and emotionalism. Since Zen is the most important philosophical tradition influencing Japanese haiku, the haiku poet aims at understanding the spirit of nature. Basho thus recognizes little division between man and nature, the subjective and the objective; he is never concerned with the problems of good and evil. A Zen poet seeks satori, the Japanese term for enlightenment. This enlightenment is defined as the state of *mu*, nothingness, which is absolutely free of any thought or emotion; it is so completely free that such a state corresponds to that of nature. For a Zen-inspired poet, nature is a mirror of the enlightened self; one must see and hear things as they really are by making one's consciousness pure and clear. Classic haiku poets like Basho, Buson, and Issa avoided expressions of good and evil, love and hate, individual feeling and collective myth; their haiku indeed shun such sentiments altogether. Their poetry was strictly concerned with the portrayal of nature—mountains, trees, flowers, birds, waterfalls, nights, days, seasons. For the Japanese haiku poet, nature reflects the enlightened self; the poet must always make his or her consciousness pure, natural, and unemotional. "Japanese poets," Noguchi wrote, "go to Nature to make life more meaningful, sing of flowers and birds to make humanity more intensive."[8]

The haiku poet may not only aim at expressing sensation but also at generalizing and hence depersonalizing it. This characteristic can be shown even by one of Basho's lesser-known haiku:

Hiya hiya to	How cool it is,
Kabe wo fumaete	Putting the feet on the wall:
Hirune kana[9]	An afternoon nap.

Basho was interested in expressing how his feet, anyone's feet, would feel when placed on the wall in the house on a warm summer afternoon. His subject was none other than this direct sensation. He did not want to convey any emotion, any thought, any beauty; there remained only poetry, only nature.

Because of its brevity and condensation, haiku seldom provides the picture with detail. The haiku poet delineates only an outline or highly selective parts and the reader must complete the vision. Above all, a classic haiku, as opposed to a modern one, is required to include a clear reference to one of the four seasons. In Basho's "The Old Pond," said to be written in the spring of 1686, a seasonal reference to spring is made by the frog in the second line: the plunging of a single frog into the deep water suddenly breaks the deadly quiet background.[10] As a result, the poet's perception of the infinitely quiet universe is intensified. It is also imperative that a haiku be primarily concerned with nature; if a haiku deals with man's life, that life must be viewed in the context of nature rather than society.

The predilection to portray man's life in association with nature means that the poet is more interested in genuinely human sentiments than in moral, ethical, or political problems. That haiku thrives upon the affinity between man and nature can be illustrated by this famous haiku by Kaga no Chiyo (1703–1775), a foremost woman poet in her age:

Asagao ni	A morning glory
Tsurube torarete	Has taken the well-bucket:
Morai mizu[11]	I'll borrow water.

Since a fresh, beautiful morning glory has grown on her well-bucket overnight, Chiyo does not mind going over to her neighbor to borrow water. Not only does her action show a desire to preserve nature, but also the poem conveys a natural and tender (as opposed to individual and personal) feeling one has for nature. A classic haiku, while it shuns human-centered emotions, thrives upon such a nature-centered feeling as Chiyo's. Nor can this sensibility be explained by logic or reason. Longer poems are often filled with intellectualized or moralized reasoning, but haiku avoids such language.

Because haiku is limited in its length, it must achieve its effect by a sense of unity and harmony within. Feelings of unity and harmony, indicative of Zen philosophy, are motivated by a desire to perceive every instant in nature and life: an intuition that nothing is alone, nothing is out of the ordinary. One of Basho's later haiku creates a sense of unity and relatedness:

Aki fukaki	Autumn is deepening:
Tonari wa nani wo	What does the neighbor do
Suru hito zo[12]	For a living?

Though a serious poet, Basho was enormously interested in commonplace and common people. In this haiku, as autumn approaches winter and he nears the end of his life, he takes a deeper interest in his fellow human beings. His observations of the season and his neighbor, a total stranger, are separate yet both observations intensify each other. His vision, as it is unified, evokes a deeply felt, natural, and universal sentiment.

In haiku, two entirely different things are joined in sameness: spirit and matter, present and future, doer and deed, word and thing, meaning and sensation. Basho's oft-quoted "A Crow" depicts a crow perching on a withered branch, a moment of reality:

Kare eda ni	A crow
Karasu no tomari taruya	Perched on a withered tree
Aki no kure[13]	In the autumn evening.

This image is followed by the coming of an autumn nightfall, a feeling of future. Present and future, thing and feeling, man and nature, each defining the other, are thus unified.

The unity of sentiment in haiku is further intensified by the poet's expression of the senses. Basho's "Sunset on the Sea," for instance, shows the unity and relatedness of the senses:

Umi kurete	Sunset on the sea:
Kamo no koe	The voices of the ducks
Honoka ni shiroshi[14]	Are faintly white.

The voices of the ducks under the darkened sky are delineated as white as well as faint. Interestingly, the chilled wind after dark evokes the whiteness associated with coldness. The voices of the ducks and the whiteness of the waves refer to two entirely different senses, but both senses, each reinforcing the other, create a unified sensation.

The transference of the senses may occur between color and mood, as shown in a haiku by Usuda Aro, a contemporary Japanese poet:

Tsuma araba	Were my wife alive,
Tozomou asagao	I thought, and saw a morning glory:
Akaki saku[15]	It has blossomed red.

The first line conveys a feeling of loneliness, but the red morning glory reminds him of a happy life they spent when she was living. The redness rather than the whiteness or blue color of the flower is transferred to the feeling of happiness and love. The transference of the senses, in turn, arouses a sense of balance and harmony. His recollection of their happy marriage, a feeling evoked by the red flower, compensates for the death of his wife, a reality.

Well-wrought haiku thrive upon the fusion of man and nature, and upon the intensity of love and beauty it creates. A haiku by Takarai Kikaku (1661–1707), Basho's first disciple and one of the most innovative poets, is exemplary:

Meigetsu ya	The harvest moon:
Tatami no uye ni	Lo, on the tatami mats
Matsu no kage[16]	The shape of a pine.

The beauty of the moonlight here is not only humanized, in that the light is shining on a man-made object, but intensified by the shadows of a pine tree that fall upon the mats. The beauty of the intricate pattern of the ageless pine tree as it stamps the dustless mats is far more luminous than the light itself. Not only does such a scene unify the image of man and the image of nature, but also man and nature interact.

During the eighteenth century a satirical form of haiku called *senryu* was developed by Karai Senryu (1718–1790) as a kind of "mock haiku" with humor, moralizing nuances, and a philosophical tone, expressing "the incongruity of things" more than their oneness, dealing more often with distortions and failures, not just with the harmonious beauty of nature, as can be seen in the following *senryu:*

> When she wails
> At the top of her voice,
> The husband gives in.[17]

Because *senryu* tend to appeal more to one's sense of the logical than to intuition, many of Wright's haiku can be read as *senryu.*

As the haiku has developed over the centuries, it has

established certain aesthetic principles. To define and illustrate them is difficult since they refer to subtle perceptions and complex states of mind in the creation of poetry. Above all, these principles are governed by the national character developed over the centuries. Having changed in meaning, they do not necessarily mean the same today as they did in the seventeenth century. Discussion of these terms, furthermore, proves difficult simply because poetic theory does not always correspond to what poets actually write. It has also been true that the aesthetic principles for the haiku are often applied to other genres of Japanese art such as Noh plays, flower arrangement, and tea ceremony.

One of the most delicate principles of Eastern art is called *yugen*. Originally *yugen* in Japanese art was an element of style pervasive in the language of Noh. It was also a philosophical principle originated in Zen metaphysics. In Zen, every individual possesses Buddhahood and must realize it. *Yugen*, as applied to art, designates the mysterious and dark, what lies under the surface. The mode of expression is subtle as opposed to obvious, suggestive rather than declarative. In reference to the *Works* by Zeami, the author of many of the extant Noh plays, Arthur Waley expounds this difficult term, *yugen:*

> It is applied to the natural graces of a boy's movements, to the gentle restraint of a nobleman's speech and bearing. "When notes fall sweetly and flutter delicately to

the ear," that is the *yugen* of music. The symbol of *yugen* is "a white bird with a flower in its beak." "To watch the sun sink behind a flower-clad hill, to wander on and on in a huge forest with no thought of return, to stand upon the shore and gaze after a boat that goes hid [*sic*] by far-off islands, to ponder on the journey of wild geese seen and lost among the clouds"—such are the gates to *yugen*.[18]

Such a scene conveys a feeling of satisfaction and release, as does the catharsis of a Greek tragedy, but *yugen* differs from catharsis because it has little to do with the emotional stress caused by tragedy. *Yugen* functions in art as a means by which man can comprehend the course of nature. Although *yugen* seems allied with a sense of resignation, it has a far different effect upon the human psyche. A certain type of Noh play like *Takasago* celebrates the order of the universe ruled by heaven. The mode of perception in the play may be compared to that of a pine tree with its evergreen needles, the predominant representation on the stage. The style of *yugen* can express either happiness or sorrow. Cherry blossoms, however beautiful they may be, must fade away; love between man and woman is inevitably followed by sorrow.

This mystery and inexplicability, which surrounds the order of the universe, had a strong appeal to a classic haiku poet like Basho. His "The Old Pond," as discussed earlier, shows that while the poet describes a natural phenomenon realistically, he conveys his instant perception that nature is infinitely deep and absolutely silent. Such attributes of nature are not ostensibly stated; they are hidden. The tranquillity of the old pond with which the poet was struck remained in the background. He did not write "The rest is quiet"; instead he wrote the third line of the verse to read: "The sound of water." The concluding image was given as a contrast to the background enveloped in quiet. Basho's mode of experience is suggestive rather than descriptive, hidden and reserved rather than overt and demonstrative. *Yugen* has all the connotations of modesty, concealment, depth, and darkness. In Zen painting, woods and bays, as well as houses and boats, are hidden; hence these objects suggest infinity and profundity. Detail and refinement, which would mean limitation and temporariness of life, destroy the sense of permanence and eternity.

Another frequently used term in Japanese poetics is *sabi*. This noun derives from the verb *sabiru* (to rust) and implies that what is described is aged. The portrait of Buddha hung in Zen temples, as the Chinese painter Lian Kai's *Buddha Leaving the Mountains* suggests, depicts the Buddha as an old man in contrast to the young figure typically shown in other temples.[19] Zen's Buddha looks emaciated, his environment barren: his body, his tattered clothes, the aged tree standing nearby, the pieces of dry wood strewn about, all indicate that they have passed the prime of their life and function. In this kind of portrait the old man with thin body is nearer to his soul as the old tree with its skin and leaves fallen is to the very origin and essence of nature.

Sabi is traditionally associated with loneliness. Aesthetically, however, this mode of sensibility smacks of grace rather than splendor; it suggests quiet beauty as opposed to robust beauty. Basho's "A Crow," quoted earlier, best illustrates this principle. Loneliness suggested by a single crow on a branch of an old tree is reinforced by the elements of time indicated by nightfall and autumn. The picture is drawn with little detail and the overall mood is created by a simple, graceful description of fact. Furthermore, parts of the picture are delineated, by implication, in dark colors: the crow is black, the branch dark brown, the background dusky. The kind of beauty associated with the loneliness in Basho's poem is in marked contrast to the robust beauty depicted in a poem by Mukai Kyorai (1651–1704), Basho's disciple:

Hana mori ya	The guardians
Shiroki katsura wo	Of the cherry blossoms
Tsuki awase[20]	Lay their white heads together.

The tradition of haiku established in the seventeenth century produced eminent poets like Buson and Issa in the eighteenth, but the revolt against this tradition took place toward the end of the nineteenth century under the banner of a young poet, Masaoka Shiki (1867–1902). On the one hand, Basho's followers, instead of becoming innovators like their master, resorted to an artificiality reminiscent of the comic *renga*; on the other hand, Issa, when he died, left no disciples. The Meiji restoration (1868) called for changes in all aspects of Japanese culture, and Shiki became a leader in the literary revolution. He launched an attack on the tradition by publishing his controversial essay, "Criticism of Basho." In response to a haiku by Hattori Ransetsu (1654–1707), Basho's disciple, Shiki composed his own. Ransetsu's haiku had been written two centuries earlier:

Ki giku shira giku	Yellow and white chrysanthemums:
Sono hoka no na wa	What other possible names?
Naku-mogana[21]	None can be thought of.

To Ransetsu's poem, Shiki responded with this one:

Ki giku shira giku	Yellow and white chrysanthemums:
Hito moto wa aka mo	But at least another one—
Aramahoshi[22]	I want a red one.

Shiki advised his followers that they compose haiku to please themselves. To Shiki, some of the conventional poems lack direct, spontaneous expressions: a traditional haiku poet in his adherence to old rules of grammar and devices such as *kireji* (cutting word), resorted to artificially twisting words and phrases.

A modernist challenge Shiki gave the art of haiku, however, kept intact such aesthetic principles as *yugen* and *sabi*. Classic poets like Basho and Issa, who adhered to such principles, were also devout Buddhists. By contrast, Shiki, while abiding by the aesthetic principles, was regarded as an agnostic: his philosophy of life is demonstrated in this haiku:

Aki kaze ya	The wind in autumn
Ware ni kami nashi	As for me, there are no gods,
Hotoke nashi[23]	There are no Buddhas.

Although Shiki's direct references to the divinities of Japanese culture resemble a modernist style, the predominant image created by "the wind in autumn," a conventional *kigo* (seasonal word), suggests a deep-seated sense of loneliness and coldness. Shiki's mode of expression in this haiku is based upon *sabi*.

Some well-known haiku poets in the twentieth century also preserve the sensibility of *sabi*. The predicament of a patient described in this haiku by Ishida Hakyo arouses *sabi*:

Byo shitsu ni	In the hospital room
Su bako tsukuredo	I have built a nest box but
Tsubame kozu[24]	Swallows never appear.

Not only do the first and third lines indicate facts of loneliness, but the patient's will to live suggested by the second line also evokes a poignant sensibility. To a modern poet like

Hakyo, the twin problems of humanity are loneliness and boredom. He sees the same problems exist in nature as this haiku by him illustrates:

Ori no washi	The caged eagle;
Sabishiku nareba	When lonely
Hautsu ka mo	He flaps his wings.

The feeling of *sabi* is also aroused by the private world of the poet, the situation others cannot envision, as this haiku by Nakamura Kusatao, another modernist, shows:

Ka no koe no	At the faint voices
Hisoka naru toki	Of the flying mosquitoes
Kui ni keri[25]	I felt my remorse.

Closely related to *sabi* is a poetic sensibility called *wabi*. Traditionally *wabi* has been defined in sharp antithesis to the folk or plebeian saying, *"Hana yori dango"* (Rice dumplings are preferred to flowers). Some poets are inspired by the sentiment that human beings desire beauty more than food, an attribute lacking in animals and other nonhuman beings. *Wabi* thus refers to the uniquely human perception of beauty stemmed from poverty. *Wabi* is often regarded as religious, as the Western saying "Blessed are the poor" suggests, but the spiritual aspect of *wabi* is based upon the aesthetic rather than the moral sensibility.

This mode of expression is often attributed to Basho, who did not come from a well-to-do family. Basho's life as an artist was that of a wandering bard as recorded in his celebrated diaries and travelogues, the most famous of which is *Oku no Hoso Michi* (*The Narrow Road of Oku*). *Nozarashi Kiko* (*A Travel Account of My Exposure in the Fields*), one of Basho's earlier books of essays, opens with this revealing passage with two haiku:

> When I set out on my journey of a thousand leagues I packed no provisions for the road. I clung to the staff of that pilgrim of old who, it is said, "entered the realm of nothingness under the moon after midnight." The voice of the wind sounded cold somehow as I left my tumbledown hut on the river in the eighth moon of the Year of the Rat, 1684.

Nozarashi wo	Bones exposed in a field—
Kokoro ni kaze no	At the thought, how the wind
Shimu mi ka na	Bites into my flesh.
Aki too tose	Autumn—this makes ten years;
Kaette Edo wo	Now I really mean Edo
Sasu kokyoo[26]	When I speak of "home."

The first haiku conveys a sense of *wabi* because the image of his bones suggests poverty and eternity. Although Basho has fallen on fatigue and hardship on his journey, he has reached a higher state of mind. The expression of *wabi* in this verse is characterized by the feelings of aging, leanness, and coldness. Basho's attachment to art rather than to provision on his travel is shown in this haiku:

Michi nobe no	Upon the roadside
Mukuge wa uma ni	Grew mallow flowers: my horse
Kuware keri[27]	Has eaten them all.

Rikyu (1521–1591), the famed artist of the tea ceremony, wrote that food which is enough to sustain body and a roof that does not leak are sufficient for man's life. For Basho, however, an empty stomach was necessary to create poetry. Among Basho's disciples, Rotsu (1651?–1739?), the beggar-poet, is well known for having come into Basho's legacy of *wabi*. This haiku by Rotsu best demonstrates his state of mind:

Tori domo mo	The water-birds too
Neitte iru ka	Are asleep
Yogo no umi[28]	On the lake of Yogo?

Rotsu portrays a scene with no sight or sound of birds on the desolate lake. The withered reeds rustle from time to time in the chilly wind. It is only Rotsu the beggar and artist who is awake and is able to capture the beauty of the lake.

The sensibilities of *yugen*, *sabi*, and *wabi* all derive from the ways in which Japanese poets have seen nature over the centuries. Although the philosophy of Zen, on which the aesthetics of a poet like Basho is based, shuns emotion and intellect altogether, haiku is nonetheless concerned with one's feeling and thought. If haiku conveys the poet's feeling, that feeling must have been aroused by nature. That the art of haiku comes from man's affinity with nature is best explained by Basho in his travelogue *Oi no Kobumi* (*Manuscript in My Knapsack*):

> One and the same thing runs through the waka of Saigyo, the renga of Sogi, the paintings of Sesshu, the tea ceremony of Rikyu. What is common to all these arts is their following nature and making a friend of the four seasons. Nothing the artist sees is but flowers, nothing he thinks of but is the moon. When what a man sees is not flowers, he is no better than a barbarian. When what he thinks in his heart is not the moon, he belongs to the same species as the birds and beasts. I say, free yourselves from the barbarian, remove yourself from the birds and beasts; follow nature and return to nature![29]

Not only does this passage reveal that Basho had great confidence in his art, but that he also believed that although the form of haiku differs from that of any other art, the essence of haiku remains the same.

II

The evidence of Wright's identification with nature and his use of its motifs stretches from "Big Boy Leaves Home," with its rural events around the swimming hole, to *Black Boy*, and it culminates in the haiku. In *Black Boy* he expresses his delight "in seeing long straight rows of red and green vegetables," or his nostalgia when he hears "the crying strings of wild geese winging south against a bleak, autumn sky." He even wishes to "imitate the petty pride of sparrows" and finds an "incomprehensible secret embodied in a whitish toadstool hiding in the dark shade of a rotting log." Most revealing, perhaps, is his yearning for identification when he sees "a solitary ant carrying a burden upon a mysterious journey."[30] The evidence is a record of his early childhood days and sensations, transformed beyond the expansive symbolism of *Black Boy* into those patterns from Mississippi days when Wright learned to identify his mood and self with specific aspects of nature. The domain of nature was a world Wright wanted to inhabit. Perhaps he did for a while when, with his wife and daughter, he lived from 1947 to 1960 on his farm in Ailly, Normandy.[31] There he liked to work afternoons in his garden.

When Wright turned to writing haiku he was certainly not working in an artistic vacuum. Artists in the Western world had been interested in haiku, its history and meaning, and had been writing haiku since early in the twentieth century. As a result of visits to Japan, French writers Julien Vocance, Paul-Louis Couchoud, and others began to write haiku in French. In 1910 a translation of a Japanese anthology of literature was made by Michael Revon, who referred to Basho's hokku as "haikai." Then in 1915 Vocance wrote a group of poems called *Cent Visions de Guerre* in the haiku form. By 1920 at least a dozen poets were writing haiku for the *Nouvelle revue française*. In London at the end of 1910, Basil Hall Chamberlain's second edition of Japanese poetry was published, with his essay "Basho and the Japanese Poetical Epigram."[32]

Soon American poets began to write haiku, the most famous, perhaps, being Ezra Pound, who wrote "In a Station of the Metro."[33] Some might consider his poem to be the first published haiku written in English. Other Americans rapidly followed Pound's lead: Wallace Stevens in 1917, William Carlos Williams in 1919, and Amy Lowell in the same year.[34] As early as 1909 the Imagist group of poets were influenced by both the tanka (a short verse form of five lines with 5,7,5,7,7 syllables respectively) and the haiku forms. The group included Ezra Pound, Amy Lowell, and John Gould Fletcher.[35] In 1915 in Boston, Lafcadio Hearn's translations of hokku and tanka were collected and published as *Japanese Lyrics*.[36] By the mid-1930s, Georges Bonneau began to publish a series of books, with his translation into French, of Japanese poetry, *Le Haiku*. English translations of Japanese haiku by Harold G. Henderson came out in 1934 as *The Bamboo Broom*.

The Second World War temporarily sidetracked the

Western world's interest in haiku. But after the war, British writers in Tokyo began to renew Western interest in haiku. The most important of these writers were Harold G. Henderson and R. H. Blyth. Their interest in haiku and subsequent books and translations once again made haiku a viable literary art form for Western poets. Blyth had studied Zen and believed that "Zen Buddhism was the dominant influence on the traditional Japanese arts, particularly haiku." His *Haiku: Volume I*, the first of four volumes, came out in 1949 and later was reissued in 1952 under the title *Haiku*.[37]

John Gould Fletcher introduced the West to Kenneth Yasuda's *A Pepper-Pod*, a translation of Japanese haiku with selections of original haiku written in English in 1946. Gary Snyder wrote haiku in his diary, published in 1952 under the title *Earth House Hold*. Allen Ginsberg read Blyth's work on haiku and started to write haiku himself. An entry in his journal reads as follows: "Haiku composed in the backyard cottage at . . . Berkeley 1955, while reading R. H. Blyth's 4 volumes *Haiku*."[38] In 1958 Harold G. Henderson's revised 1930 work, retitled *An Introduction to Haiku*, appeared in America and generated more interest in haiku. Another influential work that year was Jack Kerouac's *The Dharma Bums*. Kerouac's character Japhy Ryder writes haiku and had read a four-volume work on Japanese haiku. This could easily be a reference to Blyth's four volumes on haiku. Anyway, hundreds of Americans began to write haiku.[39]

Harold G. Henderson, in *An Introduction to Haiku*, gives thanks to R. H. Blyth, with whom he had had personal contact, and refers to Blyth's "monumental four-volume work on haiku."[40] And William J. Higginson, in *The Haiku Handbook*, refers to the American writer Richard Wright and says that he had studied R. H. Blyth's books and "wrote several hundred haiku during the last year and a half of his life."[41]

In 1953 Wright traveled to Africa and published *Black Power* the following year. In 1955 he attended the Bandung Conference of the Third World; two years later he was a member of the First Congress of Negro Artists and Writers, which met in Paris in September. During that same period he liked to work in his garden on his Normandy farm,[42] an activity that supplied many themes for his haiku.

The decade of the 1950s was rich in possibilities for Wright. The Third World was coming into its own artistically, socially, and politically, and Wright was gradually shedding his romantic belief that in denying men the chance to act on the basis of their feelings, social institutions cause the individual to destroy such feelings.[43] But set against this positive mood were the effects of his financial and personal problems. His works were not bringing in much money, nor had he written anything in the previous few years that was financially successful. In addition, by the beginning of 1959 he was sick and often confined to his bed. He was approaching the end of the decade in an ambivalent mood, ready for union with that which lies beyond the artist, a theme appropriate for haiku. Exhausted by his financial problems, sickness, and the polemics surrounding him that were a drain on his rational powers, Wright was mentally and emotionally receptive to the ideas, beauty, and form of haiku. Under these conditions he seemed to be liberated from the restrictions of rationality and to enjoy his intuitive responses to other powers and images latent within him.

Sometime during the summer of 1959 he had been introduced to haiku by a young South African friend who loved its form.[44] Wright borrowed from him R. H. Blyth's four volumes on the art of haiku and its relationship to Zen and settled down to rediscover his old dream of oneness with all life. By March 1960 he was so captivated by its beauty that he was already in the midst of composing what was to turn out to be almost four thousand separate haiku. In response to a letter from his friend and Dutch translator, Margrit de Sablonière, he said that he had returned to poetry and added, "During my illness I experimented with the Japanese form of poetry called haiku; I wrote some 4,000 of them and am now sifting them out to see if they are any good."

In his discussion of this event, Michel Fabre notes that Wright's interest in haiku involved his research into the great Japanese masters, Buson, Basho, and Issa. Wright ignored the European and American forms that were then becoming popular. Fabre notes further that Wright made "an effort to respect the exact form of the poem," and adds that it was curious for Wright to become interested in haiku at a time when he was fighting his illness. As Fabre reasons, "Logically he should have been tempted to turn away from 'pure' literature and to use his pen instead as a weapon."[45] Just as curiously, Wright's biographer Constance Webb refers to none of this material. She merely says that Wright had lost his physical energy and that "while lying against the pillows one afternoon he picked up the small book of Japanese poetry and began to read it again." Apparently it had been given to him earlier, and he read and reread it, excited by its style. She comments that Wright "had to study it and study to find out why it struck his ear with such a modern note." Then she adds that Wright "would try to bring the life and consciousness of a black American" to its form. Again according to Webb, the haiku "seemed to answer the rawness he felt, which had, in turn, created a sensitivity that ached. Never had he been so sensitive, as if his nervous system had been exposed to rough air." In a letter to Paul Reynolds, his friend and editor, Wright said that he had sent to William Targ of the World Publishing Company a manuscript of his haiku.[46] In that same letter he commented that "these poems are the results of my being in bed a great deal. . . ."[47]

Until we read the poems in *Haiku: This Other World* and his unpublished haiku we will probably never know the other reasons why Wright turned to haiku during the last years of his life. But that knowledge, while helpful, is not necessary to reread and enjoy these newly published haiku. What is necessary, both for enjoyment and understanding of

Wright's haiku, is some knowledge about haiku as the great Japanese poets developed the genre. For this, see Part I of Afterword.

In "Blueprint for Negro Writing," Wright wrote that "the Negro writer who seeks to function within his race as a purposeful agent has a serious responsibility. In order to do justice to his subject matter, in order to depict Negro life in all of its manifold and intricate relationships, a deep, informed, and complex consciousness is necessary; a consciousness which draws for its strength upon the fluid lore of a great people, and moulds this lore with the concepts that move and direct the forces of history today." Despite the context of that idea, drawn from a discussion of "Social Consciousness and Responsibility," the concept of an individual consciousness dependent on the "fluid lore" of a people raises, as Wright noted, "the question of the personality of the writer. It means that in the lives of Negro writers must be found those materials and experiences which will create a meaningful picture of the world today." Wright felt that in his new role the black writer must "create values by which his race is to struggle, live and die." In his discussion of "The Problem of Theme," he adds that "this does not mean that a Negro writer's sole concern must be with rendering the social scene"; instead, he must have a sense of "the whole life" that "he is seeking" and that needs to be "vivid and strong in him."[48]

What was "vivid and strong" in Wright, and had been from childhood on, was the haiku moment—the *where*, the *when*, and the *what*—not that he in his early years would have called it that. Being a responsible agent for his people meant that Wright had to draw on the materials of his own life, much of which was deeply involved with his feelings about nature. To have a sense of "the whole life" and "create values" for his people meant that Wright had to contend with his deepest yearnings about a harmonious union between people and nature. In haiku he must have found echoes of all he believed in and desired, both in the form, which was pleasurable and challenging to him as an artist, and in the content, so strongly appealing to his inner self. In the haiku moment he found his best self.

Joan Giroux says that the haiku moment "may be defined as an instant in which man becomes united to an object, virtually becomes that object and realizes the eternal, universal truth contained in being." In quoting from the poet Kenneth Yasuda's point of view about the moment, she adds that the writer of haiku " 'in a brief moment . . . sees a pattern, a significance he had not seen before.' "[49] In his own discussion about Wright's poetry, Michel Fabre points out, commenting on the "hymns to nature" in *12 Million Black Voices*, that "the symbolism leads to the discovery of a metaphysical reality in the scene before the poet's eyes. Poetry no longer appears as a creation—as it did in 'Old Habit and New Love'—but as a revelation. The poetic moment becomes an epiphany."[50]

Wright's "poetic moment" may not be as sharply and

traditionally defined as it is for the great Japanese writers of haiku, but it grew out of his childhood relations with nature, as Fabre has gone to some pains to reveal. To the themes of black suffering, desire for interracial unity, and the triumph of socialism, Wright added "a keen sensitivity to nature," grounding his lyricism in personal experiences. In his early poems, such as "Everywhere Burning Waters Rise," the references to nature focus on its destructive aspects. But in "We of the Streets," another early poem, Wright borrows from nature and begins, according to Fabre, to use nature as the "touchstone of his poetic sensitivity: it was the Mississippi country that restored his strength during a childhood of struggle and deprivation."

Wright's tendency to see himself set against the background of nature was strongly influenced by his love for Carl Sandburg's and Walt Whitman's poetry. Thus he made his own poetry "the vehicle of his enthusiasm or his indignation." In *12 Million Black Voices*, however, for the first time he began to use an imagery that links the individual with nature, comparing children to black buttercups. As Fabre comments, "Here evocation and image are one; the lyricism springs from an open sympathy long considered the distinctive trait of Negro sensitivity and the psychological foundation of negritude. It is in the childhood memories of the author that this lyricism has its root, memories that will be revived in the autobiographical *Black Boy*." That all of this is important in leading up to the writing of the haiku Fabre clearly understands. In discussing *12 Million Black Voices*, Fabre refers to the nostalgia that Wright developed in the lines, and then observes, "The sense of universality is suggested by simply the sight of the birds' flight. This is exactly what will occur in the haiku that Wright composed in the final stages of his poetic evolution."[51]

The haiku moment is the heart of haiku because it links complementary and antithetical qualities; that is, directness and paradox, austerity and joy, love of nature and the ordinary. It is an expression in words of "the instant of intuition uniting poet and object."[52] Wright achieves this rare quality, the haiku moment, in an excellent poem (571):

> From across the lake,
> Past the black winter trees,
> Faint sounds of a flute.

The visual image of blackness, trees, lake, and winter is joined with the aural image of a manmade sound from the flute. Two kinds of life become one in the setting placed in the distance. Everything is muted by the adjective "faint," which seems to stress quietness as the natural condition of man, trees with the lake, and winter as provider of a sense of place and time. All nature is unified with human beings through the poet's perception and expression, but the author's personality seems almost imperceptible. The quality of the haiku cannot bear too much sound or thought, either of which would increase the tone of the flute and force human beings and their philosophizing to dominate the scene.

As Joan Giroux says, quoting from Kenneth Yasuda, " 'The intent of all haiku and the discipline of the form' is to render the haiku moment, to express the 'ah-ness.' "[53] In linking directness and paradox, the essential aspects of haiku indicate that the poet needs to look straight at things and to transform the perception into words that do not depend upon metaphors or symbols.[54] Rather, the poet should present the event or object nude, so as to form a doorway for the mind. The paradox results from the simultaneity of two different things being perceived as one through the response of the poet, an effect that cannot be expressed solely through individual words. But the ability to reject metaphor and symbol did not come easily to Wright. Much more at hand was his own preoccupation with the black and white meanings in his life, a concern that becomes an effective theme in his haiku. In haiku 226:

> Like a spreading fire,
> Blossoms leap from tree to tree
> In a blazing spring.

and in haiku 1:

> I am nobody:
> A red sinking autumn sun
> Took my name away.

Wright interjects such anthropomorphic characteristics and metaphors as leaping blossoms and a sun that takes one's name, making them elements of the natural world that reflect how the speaker assigns the vegetative world animal characteristics or makes it sympathize with him. In haiku 226 the speaker provides "blossoms" with the ability of a squirrel or cougar, and in the last example above he turns the red autumn sun into a symbol, perhaps of the Western world, America, which has deprived the speaker of his name and identity, perhaps that of a black African.

In these haiku Wright supplies the *where* and *when*, an orchard setting, a season of spring, a vague place in autumn. The approach is indirect, with the meanings coming from within the poet. Behind symbol and metaphor Wright seems to hide the depth of his personal feelings, as he does in haiku 31:

> In the falling snow
> A laughing boy holds out his palms
> Until they are white.

Although the speaker is not directly in the scene, the poem presents one of Wright's favorite themes through the emphasized use of the word "white," indirectly through reference to snow and directly through a description of the boy's hands. But the effect of describing the boy as laughing creates a question: Why is he laughing? The possible answers drive one to consider the possibility that the boy's hands are not originally white. In either case, whether the boy is white or black and is laughing because of sheer delight or because he has become white for a moment, the term "white" has symbolic overtones not present in "snow," "falling," "boy," or "palms."

As for paradox, Wright clearly was experimenting. In an excellent haiku (455) Wright captures the paradox of color and shape of two separate things, one a cocklebur and one a black boy:

> The green cockleburs
> Caught in the thick wooly hair
> Of the black boy's head.

The two objects, disparate in shape, size, and color are held together by one quality both share: the matching texture of the boy's hair and the cockleburs, as perceived by the poet. By chance in a moment of intuition, two aspects of nature, two forms of life are seen as one without the poet naturalizing the boy or humanizing the burr. In this haiku Wright has presented in direct statement the paradox of union, expressing the desire to be a part of nature while simultaneously maintaining one's separate identity. Although the *where* is vague, someplace in nature, the *when* is summer before the time of ripeness, and the *what* is the sense of complete harmony with nature.

As for austerity and joy, Wright as an artist must have

struggled to develop these characteristics in his haiku. Austerity refers to the absence of philosophical or metaphysical comment, the absence of intellectualization or imposition of an excessive rationality. It calls for a simplicity of language, thought, and image, a lack of complication often revealed in the spontaneous joy of union. As R. H. Blyth says, the joy comes from the "(apparent) re-union of ourselves with things."[55] It is the "happiness of being our true selves."[56] Austerity is not only a lack of intellectualization, it is almost a wordlessness, a condition in which words are used not to externalize a poet's state of feeling, but to "clear away something," according to Blyth, "that seems to stand between" the poet and real things. Because the real things are not actually separate from the poet, they "are then perceived by self-knowledge." Certainly, haiku ideally removes as many words as possible, stressing non-intellectuality, as thought, like passion, must depend upon and not substitute for intuition. The joy lies in the humor, the lightness, the lack of sentimentality. Blyth states: "It goes down to something deeper than the unconscious where repressions wait with ill-concealed impatience. It goes beyond this into the realm where a thing is and is not at the same time, and yet at the very same time *is*."[57]

In a good haiku (22) that presents a Zen kind of humor,

> With a twitching nose
> A dog reads a telegram
> On a wet tree trunk.

the austerity and joy are central. The language is simple. Except for "telegram," all are native English words, most being one-syllable words. The poem has a simplicity unadorned with sentimentalism or sententious comment. It is the season of rain in a place of dogs and trees. Ironically, the metaphor "telegram" unites the elements of nature, the tree, and the dog with a construction of human beings—a telegram—through the personification embodied in "reads." Here Wright maintains some intellectual distance by refusing to elaborate, to go beyond the idea of a telegram with its sense of a code in communication, chemical for the dog, and electrical for people. The humor lies in the visual image of the dog twitching his nose, especially in "twitching," which carries a double meaning: one is visual, suggesting how the dog comes in contact with—that is, reads—his message; the other, also visual, suggests a sense of the sharpness of the message, the odor, that causes a slight physical movement. Thus the key terms "telegram" and "reads" are central to the poem.

The last major characteristic of the haiku moment is a love of nature that is inseparable from the ordinary. A love of nature without humanizing or sentimentalizing it stems from the Taoist belief in the unity and harmony of all things, a sense of kinship between all things, reflecting at times an irony which derives from the paradox that the more one learns, the more that knowledge tends to abolish the arbitrary division between man and nature.[58] For

R. H. Blyth this characteristic is explained in terms of self-lessness, meaning that the poet has identified with nature. The loss of his individuality within the union involves a generalized melancholy aspect or loneliness as an underlying rhythm. It represents a state of Zen, of "absolute spiritual poverty in which, having nothing, we possess all." We rejoice with those who rejoice, weep with those who weep, are moved as all things in nature are moved, by the same forces—the inevitability of nature.[59]

Such concepts are also part of the idea of materiality that suffuses haiku, in which the material or the concrete is emphasized without the expression of any general principles or abstract reasoning. Animate and inanimate lose their differences to such an extent that one can say that haiku are about things. In this almost stoical sense, the ordinary thing and the love of nature are reduced to a detached love of life as it is, without idealistic, moralistic, or ethical attachments. Things are equal to human beings; both exist through and because of each other.[60] These ideas are apparent in Wright's snail haiku (7), though it is perhaps closer to being a *senryu* than a true haiku:

> Make up your mind, Snail!
> You are half inside your house,
> And halfway out!

Wright's poem presents a consideration of a simple living thing from nature through the poet's perception of the visual scene.

Despite the large number of haiku that he wrote, it was difficult for Wright to master in such a short time—a year perhaps—the complexities of haiku. Many of these haiku represent his best poetry, but he never totally learned to eliminate his political and personal attitudes in them. Clearly he was experimenting with his own African-American approach to the haiku form. Constance Webb is correct in saying that to this uniquely Japanese form of poetry Wright was trying "to bring the life and consciousness of a black American." He was not only writing out of the themes and desires that filled his earlier work, he was writing out of his loneliness. He explained to his friend Margrit de Sablonière: "I'd like to be alone, as much alone as possible. Have you taken up solitude for your friend? I have. When I'm alone and wake up in the morning, with my world of dreams close by me, I write without effort. By noon, I've done a day's work. All else, after that, is gravy, as the Americans say."[61] Wright never tired of trying to fuse his two dreams—of black union with white and of his personal symbolical union with nature.

The major themes in Wright's haiku reveal his desire to create another world in which his black and white focus would be part of his feeling for nature. He writes most often about death and the setting sun, about the moon and loneliness, about scarecrows, the rain, about farms and farm animals, about birds and insects, and about spring, the season of blossoms and blooming magnolias. In the following haiku (508), for example,

> It is September,
> The month in which I was born;
> And I have no thoughts.

he offers the *when*. It is September, a time that has special meaning for the poet-speaker. It is not only his birth month, but it is associated with specific behavior that is supposed to occur on one's birthday or during that month. There seems to be no *where*, no place, no concept of nature. The poem anchors itself to a rational process that can be summarized by saying, "It is my birthday; one has thoughts (about the past or oneself?) on one's birthday; but I have no thoughts." What seems to emerge from the poem is a sense of the passing of a creative mood in which his creativity is associated with the fall season and its cyclical overtones. Both the poet and the year seem to be in a quiescent phase, part of a cycle preparing for sleep or death.

Similarly, in 425,

> An empty sickbed:
> An indented white pillow
> In weak winter sun.

the theme of death in a white world under a weak sun emerges strongly. Death and its associations with bones and graveyards occur frequently in Wright's haiku. In 172,

> The scarecrow's old hat
> Was flung by the winter wind
> Into a graveyard.

and in 698,

> Black winter hills
> Nibbling at the sinking sun
> With stark stumpy teeth.

Wright combines death with winter, with a sinking sun (his personal symbol). He also associates death with birds, which he so frequently writes about, and with tombstones, as in the following haiku (142 and 145):

> A wounded sparrow
> Sinks in a clear cold lake water,
> Its eyes still open.

and

> A bright glowing moon
> Pouring out its radiance
> Upon tall tombstones.

A second major theme is the relationship between nature and people based on nostalgia for a lost past, a transference of feeling from poet to nature, a sense of loneliness, or the desire for a quest. Sometimes in relating nature to people, Wright draws on the domestic world for his images, as in 57:

> Sleety rain at night
> Seasoning swelling turnips
> With a tangy taste.

and 66:

> A freezing night wind
> Wafts the scent of frying fish
> From the waterfront.

The visual images of rain, night, wind, turnips, frying fish reveal a time of nature pleasant with its associations to tangy taste and scent, associations that tend to contradict the opening lines with their references to sleep and freezing. Both poems suggest the separation of the speaker from nature and a movement into memory.

Loneliness never seems far removed from memory, however. One of Wright's often repeated ending lines is the phrase "How lonely it is," as in 574:

Standing in the crowd
In a cold drizzling rain,—
How lonely it is.

or 569:

A thin waterfall
Dribbles the whole autumn night,—
How lonely it is.

A good haiku relating loneliness with mountains and twilight
is 723:

In the afterglow
A snow-covered mountain peak
Sings of loneliness.

The same sense of loneliness and separation coupled
with nostalgia or an unstated desire occurs in 69:

Whose town did you leave,
O wild and droning spring rain,
And where do you go?

The visual image of wild rain is set within a frame of ques-
tions that generate a quality of loneliness as Wright associ-
ates his feelings with nature. There is also a lovely though

sad feeling that emerges from "wild and droning spring rain," emphasizing not a destructive but a creative aspect of things.

Often Wright identifies himself closely with some aspect of nature directly or indirectly. More commonly, he selects an element of nature whose characteristics, he emphasizes in the haiku, resemble similar ones in him. For example, in a fine haiku (117),

> The crow flew so fast
> That he left his lonely caw
> Behind in the fields.

Wright creates the impression on the surface of a pastoral setting with fields and a crow. The bird's characteristics are blackness and flight coupled with the quality "fast" and his caw, which is "lonely." The poem thus reveals color, sound, and movement. The term "lonely," applicable to the crow only if one anthropomorphizes the bird, suggests that Wright has externalized his state of mind and memory through the crow, seeming to identify with it in terms of color, movement (Wright living in various places, especially during his childhood), and loss of something, the caw or voice, that is lonely. Just as the crow outflew his caw, so Wright outstripped his childhood voice in nature, his own sense of what he was in rural Mississippi. This aspect of Wright's feelings is echoed hauntingly in one of his scarecrow haiku (684) where he identifies closely with the scarecrow, which has special meaning for him:

> As my delegate,
> The scarecrow looks pensively
> Into spring moonlight.

And it is echoed in another haiku (577) where he addresses the scarecrow directly, asking,

> Scarecrow, who starved you,
> Set you in that icy wind,
> And then forgot you?

Wright is, however, quite capable of separating his social and political responses to his own life from his reaction to nature. He wrote literally scores of haiku about animals, birds, and insects, from cats, rats, dogs, cows, snails, to sparrows, buzzards, crows, geese, and even crickets, spiders, and butterflies. He writes about their setting, their habitats, the farms of his memory and of his immediate experience in Normandy. A fine haiku (47), more in the Japanese sense than in the Western mode, is:

> The spring lingers on
> In the scent of a damp log
> Rotting in the sun.

Three different kinds of images come together through and in the poet. The visual images of the damp log and of the sun, along with the vague image of spring, are closely related through prepositional patterns with the thermal image of warmth from the sun and the rotting log, as well as with the olfactory image in the odor of the log. The poet's intuitive perception of spring is thus the interaction of all five images. The poem reveals the paradoxical union of three seemingly disparate processes of nature with a fourth: man, the moisture in the log, the warmth of the sun, and the rotting process. In effect spring is suddenly perceived as being part of decay, a recycling process, not death but a creative pattern.

Humor is also a part of Wright's theme in his relationship with nature, as evidenced in a haiku (175) with a gentle whimsical Zen humor of its own:

> Coming from the woods,
> A bull has a lilac sprig
> Dangling from a horn.

In this poem the *when* and *where* are clearly apparent; it is springtime for lilacs and a farm for the woods and bull. But the *what*, or moment, lies in the harmonious union of the images and their paradoxical relationships in the poet's sudden perception. The three visual images—the woods for a generalized sense of nature, the bull for the sense of the strong, vital male animal, and the lilac sprig—provide a sense of spring and nature associated with flowers, beauty, and sadness. The potential danger or destructiveness of the bull and his horns is thrust into the background. Their threat seems to be lessened through the humor of the visual image of the flower dangling from the bull's horn. What Wright has done is to perceive suddenly how the dangerous aspect of nature can become harmless and humorously casual in relationship to other aspects.

An equally humorous haiku (401) is one about a dog:

> A thin mangy dog
> Curls up to sleep in the dust
> Of a moonlit road.

The ordinary image of a dog in ill health sleeping on a dusty road is gently lessened by the romantic associations of moonlight. The dog who could not care less, the dusty yet attractive setting, the moonlight seem united in the poet's perception. All things become one, gaining and losing importance at the same time, a theme echoed in one of Wright's wild geese haiku (600):

> Crying out the end
> Of a long summer's sun, →
> Departing wild geese.

The theme of nature, drawn not only from his immediate experiences on his farm in Normandy, his view out a window from his sickbed, and from childhood memories of Mississippi, echoes throughout many of Wright's haiku. This is especially evident in 759:

> Like remembering,
> The hills are dim and distant
> In the winter air.

While Wright's memory might have been distant, it certainly was not dim. Nor was his love of magnolias faint. Several of his haiku contain references to or are built around magnolias or plum trees, as in 28:

> In the summer haze:
> Behind magnolias,
> Faint sheets of lightning.

or in 50:

> One magnolia
> Landed upon another
> In the dew-wet grass.

and 660:

> Between night and dawn,
> A plum tree apologized
> With profuse petals.

The relationships with plum trees and magnolias are always rich and thick with nuances set against simple but fundamental aspects of nature. The dew-wet grass, lightning, the morning hours of darkness are scenes that became part of Wright's perception of nature, past and present, as much as farm life must have been for him, as witness the following haiku (62):

> A lance of spring sun
> Falls upon the moldy oats
> In a musty barn.

There is in some of these nature haiku a scent of sadness, like the remembrance of the perfume a man's first love might have worn. Nature is cyclical; its beauty and power come and go, often reflected in a person's memory and awareness. One can only wonder what mood Wright was in, for example, when he composed the following haiku (783):

> I cannot find it,
> That very first violet
> Seen from my window.

It is a delightfully simple haiku, capturing the inadequacies existing between vision from inside and that from outside, a loss of perspective that leads one in a new direction.

Like the Japanese poet Basho, Wright had achieved in many of these haiku, which he selected himself for publication, the sense of sad oneness in nature, coupled with an ironic smile of joy and compassion. He had learned to create, as it were, his own Wordsworthian "spots of time," seeing into the life of things. In September 1960, Wright declared that he had "finished nothing this year but those damned haiku. . . ."[62] But that was enough, because in the many fine haiku that emerged from his thousands, he had found his moment, his time, his place, his union, peaceful and complete, with some aspect of life, his other world. Even if it was not with a white America, it was with a nature that had dominated his childhood and had remained forever powerful in all of his work.

On November 28, 1960, Richard Wright died at the age of 52. His daughter, Julia, reading through the haiku in manuscript after the funeral, felt this one (647) would speak for his legacy:

> Burning out its time,
> And timing its own burning,
> One lonely candle.[63]

The major image in this haiku does not come from nature, which Wright sought unconsciously and consciously all his life; it comes from the world of manmade things, the other world of poetic images. Like all things, however, it is subject to the changes of nature, and, like people, it is also capable of speeding up the process. Wright's haiku reveal more clearly than his great novels or polemical tracts his sympathetic awareness of the complex relationship between people and nature—that a person needs to know *where* he or she is going, *when* one will reach the destination, and *what* one will be when that happens.

III

A reading of the selections in *Haiku: This Other World*, as well as the rest of Wright's haiku, indicates that Wright, turning away from the moral, intellectual, social, and political problems dealt with in his prose work, found in nature his latent poetic sensibility. Above all, his fine pieces of poetry show, as do classic Japanese haiku, the unity and harmony of all things, the sensibility that man and nature are one and inseparable. While his prose exhibits a predilection for a rational world created by human beings out of the concept of their narcissistic image of themselves, humanism expressed in his haiku means more than a fellowship of human beings. It means an awareness of what human beings share with all living things. To create a human image in his haiku is to experience harmony with life at its deepest level.

The primacy of the spirit of nature over the strife of man is pronounced in Wright's later work, especially *Black Power*. In "Blueprint for Negro Writing," one of his theoretical principles calls for an African-American writer's exploration of universal humanism, what is common among all cultures. "Every iota of gain in human thought and sensibility," Wright argues, "should be ready grist for his mill, no matter how far-fetched they may seem in their immediate implications." After a journey into the Ashanti kingdom in West Africa in 1953, he wrote in *Black Power:*

> The truth is that the question of how much of Africa has survived in the New World is misnamed when termed "African survivals." The African attitude toward life springs from a natural and poetic grasp of existence and all the emotional implications that such an attitude carries; it is clear, then, that what the anthropologists have been trying to explain are not "African survivals" at all—they are but the retention of basic and primal attitudes toward life.[64]

Wright's exploration of the Ashanti convinced him that the defense of African culture meant renewal of Africans' faith in themselves. He realized for the first time that African culture was buttressed by universal human values—such as awe of nature, family kinship and love, faith in religion, and a sense of honor. For the purpose of writing haiku, this primal outlook on life, witnessed in Africa, had a singular influence on his poetic vision.

Before discussing Ashanti culture, he quotes a passage from Edmund Husserl's *Ideas*, which suggests that the world of nature dominates the scientific vision of that world—the preeminence of intuition over knowledge in the search for truth. Similarly, Wright's interpretation of the African philosophy recalls a teaching in Zen Buddhism. Unlike the other sects of Buddhism, Zen teaches that every individual possesses Buddhahood and all he or she must do is to realize it. One must purge one's mind and heart of any materialistic thoughts or feelings, and appreciate the wonder of the world here and now. Zen is a way of self-discipline and self-reliance. Its emphasis on self is derived from the prophetic admonishment Gautama Buddha is said to have given to his disciples: "Seek within, you are the Buddha." Satori, as noted earlier, is an enlightenment that transcends time and place, and even the consciousness of self. In the African primal outlook upon existence, a person's consciousness, as Wright explains, corresponds to the spirit of nature.

In Zen, if the enlightened person sees a tree, for instance, the person sees the tree through his or her enlightened eye. The tree is no longer an ordinary tree; it now exists with different meaning. In other words, the tree contains satori only when the viewer is enlightened. From a similar point of view, Wright saw in African life a closer relationship between human beings and nature than that between human beings and their social and political environment:

Africa, with its high rain forest, with its stifling heat and lush vegetation, might well be mankind's queerest laboratory. Here instinct ruled and flowered without be-

---

ing concerned with the nature of the physical structure of the world; man lived without too much effort; there was nothing to distract him from concentrating upon the currents and countercurrents of his heart. He was thus free to project out of himself what he thought he was. Man has lived here in a waking dream, and, to some extent, he still lives here in that dream.[65]

Africa evokes "a total attitude toward life, calling into question the basic assumptions of existence," just as Zen teaches a way of life completely independent of what one has been socially and politically conditioned to lead. As if echoing the enlightenment in Zen, Wright says: "Africa is the world of man; if you are wild, Africa's wild; if you are empty, so's Africa."[66]

Wright's discussion of the African concept of life is also suggestive of Zen's emphasis on transcending the dualism of life and death. Zen master Dogen (1200–1254), whose work *Shobogenzo* is known in Japan for his practical application rather than his theory of Zen doctrine, observed that since life and death are beyond human control, there is no need to avoid them. Dogen's teaching is a refutation of the assumption that life and death are entirely separate entities, as are seasons.[67] The Ashanti funeral service Wright saw showed him that "the 'dead' live side by side with the living; they eat, breathe, laugh, hate, love, and continue doing in the world of ghostly shadows exactly what they had been doing in the world of flesh and blood,"[68] a portrayal of life and death reminiscent of Philip Freneau's "Indian Burial."

Wright was, moreover, fascinated by the African reverence for the nonhuman living, a primal African attitude that corresponds to the Buddhist belief. He observed:

> The pre-Christian African was impressed with the littleness of himself and he walked the earth warily, lest he disturb the presence of invisible gods . . . he dared not cut down a tree without first propitiating its spirit so that it would not haunt him; he loved his fragile life and he was convinced that the tree loved its life also.[69]

The concept of unity, continuity, and infinity underlying that of life and death is what the Akan religion in the Ashanti kingdom and Buddhism share.[70] Indeed, Wright's reading of the African mind conforms to both religions in their common belief that humankind is not at the center of the universe. It is this revelatory and emulating relationship nature holds for human beings that makes the African primal outlook upon life akin to Zen Buddhism.

Traditionally, haiku, in its portrayal of man's association with nature, often conveys a kind of enlightenment, a new way of looking at man and nature. In some of the haiku, as the following examples indicate, Wright follows this tradition:

> A wilting jonquil
> Journeys to its destiny
> In a shut bedroom.

Lines of winter rain
Gleam only as they flash past
My lighted window.

"A Wilting Jonquil" (720) teaches the poet a lesson that nature out of its environment cannot exhibit its beauty. In "Lines of Winter Rain" (722), the poet learns that only when an interaction between man and nature occurs can natural beauty be savored.

This revelatory tradition, derived from Zen philosophy, informs many of Wright's haiku. Several of the pieces Wright selected and included toward the end of *Haiku: This Other World* reflect his conscious effort to emulate the Asian philosophy. For example, in 721,

As my anger ebbs,
The spring stars grow bright again
And the wind returns.

Wright tries to attain a state of mind called *mu*, nothingness, by controlling his emotion. This state of nothingness, however, is not synonymous with a state of void, but leads to what Wright calls, in *Black Power*, "a total attitude toward life."[71] "So violent and fickle," he writes, "was nature that [the African] could not delude himself into feeling that he, a mere man, was at the center of the universe."[72] In this haiku, as Wright relieves himself of anger, he begins to see the stars "grow bright again" and "the wind" return. Only when he attains a state of nothingness and a total attitude toward life can he perceive nature with his enlightened senses. How closely this perception of nature is related to his latent interest in the Asian philosophy can also be seen in the following:

> Why did this spring wood
> Grow so silent when I came?
> What was happening?

This haiku (809) suggests the kind of questions asked by a Zen master who teaches ways of attaining the state of *mu*. Wright here tries to give an admonition, as he does in many of his other haiku, that only with the utmost attention human beings pay nature can they truly see themselves.

Writing four thousand haiku at the end of his life was a reflection of change in his career as a writer. But, more important, the new point of view and the new mode of expression he acquired in writing haiku suggest that Wright was convinced more than ever that materialism and its corollary, greed, were the twin culprits of racial conflict. Just as his fiction and nonfiction directly present this conviction, his haiku as racial discourse indirectly express the same conviction.

NOTES

1. Poetry by Emerson and Whitman has an affinity with Japanese haiku in terms of their attitude toward nature. See Yoshinobu Hakutani, "Emerson, Whitman, and Zen Buddhism," *Midwest Quarterly* 31 (Summer 1990), 433–48.

2. The translation of this verse and other Japanese poems quoted in this book, unless otherwise noted, is by Yoshinobu Hakutani.

3. Donald Keene, *World within Walls: Japanese Literature of the Pre-Modern Era, 1600–1868* (New York: Grove Press, 1976), 13.

4. A detailed historical account of *haikai* poetry is given in Donald Keene, *World within Walls*, 337–55.

5. A certain group of poets, including Ito Shintoku (1634–1698) and Ikenishi Gonsui (1650–1722) of the Teitoku school, and Uejima Onitsura (1661–1738), Konishi Raizan (1654–1716), and Shiinomoto Saimaro (1656–1738) of the Danrin school, each contributed to refining Basho's style (Keene, 56–70).

6. The translation of this haiku is by Yone Noguchi. See Yone Noguchi, *Selected English Writings of Yone Noguchi: An East-West Literary Assimilation*, ed. Yoshinobu Hakutani (Cranbury, N.J.: Associated University Presses, 1992), Vol. II, 73–74.

7. Noguchi, *Selected English Writings*, Vol. II, 74.

8. Ibid., 69.

9. The original of "How Cool It Is" is quoted from Harold G. Henderson, *An Introduction to Haiku* (New York: Doubleday/Anchor, 1958), 49.

10. Although the frog traditionally is a *kigo* (seasonal reference) to spring, Yone Noguchi interprets "The Old Pond" as an autumnal haiku: "The Japanese mind turns it into high poetry (it is said that Basho the author instantly awoke to a knowledge of the true road his own poetry should tread with this frog poem; it has been regarded in some quarters as a thing almost sacred although its dignity is a little fallen of late) . . . because it draws at once a

picture of an autumnal desolation reigning on an ancient temple pond. . . ."
(*Selected English Writings*, Vol. II, 74).

11. The original of "A Morning Glory" is quoted from Fujio Akimoto, *Haiku Nyumon* (Tokyo: Kadokawa, 1971), 23.

12. The original of "Autumn Is Deepening" is quoted from Noichi Imoto, *Basho: Sono Jinsei to Geijitsu* (Tokyo: Kodansha, 1968), 231.

13. The original of "A Crow" is quoted from Imoto, *Basho*, p. 86. The English version is quoted from R. H. Blyth, *A History of Haiku* (Tokyo: Hokuseido, 1963–1964), Vol. II, xxix. The middle line in a later version of the poem reads: *"Karasu no tomari keri"* (Henderson, *Introduction to Haiku*, 18). The earlier version has a syllabic measure of 5,10,5, while the later version has 5,9,5 syllables, both in an unusual pattern.

14. The original of "Sunset on the Sea" is quoted from Imoto, *Basho*, 117.

15. The original of "Were My Wife Alive" is quoted from Akimoto, *Haiku Nyumon*, 200.

16. The original of "The Harvest Moon" is quoted from *"Meigetsu ya tatami-no ue ni matsu-no-kage"* (Henderson, *Introduction to Haiku*, 58).

17. Joan Giroux, *The Haiku Forum* (Rutland, Vt.: Tuttle, 1974), 22–23.

18. Arthur Waley, *The No Plays of Japan* (New York: Grove Press, 1920), 21–22.

19. See Max Loehr, *The Great Paintings of China* (New York: Harper & Row, 1980), 216.

20. The original and translation of "The Guardians" is quoted from Blyth, *History of Haiku*, Vol II, vii.

21. The original of Ransetsu's "Yellow and White Chrysanthemums" is quoted from Henderson, *Introduction to Haiku*, 160.

22. The original of Shiki's "Yellow and White Chrysanthemums" is quoted from Henderson, *Introduction to Haiku*, 160.

23. The original of "The Wind in Autumn" is quoted from Henderson, *Introduction to Haiku*, 164.

24. The original of "In the Hospital Room" is quoted from Akimoto, *Haiku Nyumon*, 222.

25. The original of "The Caged Eagle" is quoted and translated by Blyth, *History of Haiku*, Vol. II, 347. The original of "At the Faint Voices" is also quoted from ibid., Vol. II, 322.

26. Quoted and translated by Keene, *World within Walls*, 81.

27. The original of "Upon the Roadside" is quoted from Keene, *World within Walls*, 85.

28. Quoted and translated by Blyth, *History of Haiku*, Vol. II, viii–ix.

29. Ibid., 93.

30. Wright, *Black Boy: A Record of Childhood and Youth* (New York: Harper, 1945), 7.

31. Michel Fabre, *The Unfinished Quest of Richard Wright* (New York: Morrow, 1973), 447.

32. William J. Higginson with Penny Harter, *The Haiku Handbook* (New York: McGraw-Hill, 1985), 49–51.

33. For the composition of this poem and Pound's indebtedness to Japanese poetics and to haiku in particular, see Yoshinobu Hakutani, "Ezra Pound, Yone Noguchi, and Imagism," *Modern Philology* 90 (August 1992), 46–69.

34. Higginson, *Haiku Handbook*, 51–52.

35. Kenneth Yasuda, *The Japanese Haiku* (Rutland, Vt.: Tuttle, 1957), xvii.

36. Higginson, *Haiku Handbook*, 51.

37. Ibid., 57–58.

38. Ibid., 58.

39. Ibid., 63–64.

40. See Henderson, *Introduction to Haiku*, xi.

41. Higginson, *Haiku Handbook*, 65.

42. Fabre, *Quest*, 375, 447.

43. Ibid., 481.

44. Ibid., 505.

45. Ibid., 505–6.

46. See Editors' Note on page xiii of this book.

47. Constance Webb, *Richard Wright* (New York: G. P. Putnam's Sons, 1968), 387, 393–94.

48. Wright, "Blueprint for Negro Writing," in *Richard Wright Reader*, eds. Ellen Wright and Michel Fabre (New York: Harper & Row, 1978), 43–44, 46.

49. Giroux, *Haiku Forum*, 46.

50. Michel Fabre, "The Poetry of Richard Wright," *Studies in Black Literature* 1 (Autumn 1970), 17.

51. Fabre, "Poetry," 13–16, 18.

52. Giroux, *Haiku Forum*, 45–47.

53. Ibid., 76.

54. Ibid., 50–51.

55. R. H. Blyth, *Haiku* (Tokyo: Hokuseido, 1949), Vol. I, viii.

56. Giroux, *Haiku Forum*, 55–59.

57. Blyth, *Haiku*, Vol. I, 190, 192–204, 214–17.

58. Giroux, *Haiku Forum*, 63–67.

59. Blyth, *Haiku*, Vol. I, 168–72.

60. Ibid., 247–56.

61. Webb, *Richard Wright*, 393–94.

62. Fabre, "Poetry," 21.

63. Webb, *Richard Wright*, 400.

64. Richard Wright, *Black Power* (New York: Harper & Brothers, 1954), 266.

65. Ibid., 159.

66. Ibid.

67. Kodo Kurebayashi, *Dogen Zen Nyumon* (Tokyo: Daiho Rinkaku, 1983), 121–29.

68. Wright, *Black Power*, 213.

69. Ibid., 261–62.

70. Interviewed by *L'Express* in 1955 shortly after the publication of *Black Power*, Wright responded to the question, "Why do you write?":

> The accident of race and color has placed me on both sides: the Western World and its enemies. If my writing has any aim, it is to try to reveal that which is human on both sides, to affirm the essential unity of man on earth.

See "Richard Wright: I Curse the Day When for the First Time I Heard the Word 'Politics,'" *L'Express*, 18 October 1955, p. 8, introductory paragraph and questions translated by Keneth Kinnamon, in *Conversations with Richard Wright*, eds. Keneth Kinnamon and Michel Fabre (Jackson: University Press of Mississippi, 1993), 163.

71. Wright, *Black Power*, 159.

72. Ibid., 262.